Sex work on the streets

Prostitutes and their clients

Sex work on the streets

Prostitutes and
their clients

Neil McKeganey and
Marina Barnard

Open University Press
Buckingham · Philadelphia

Open University Press
Celtic Court
22 Ballmoor
Buckingham
MK18 1XW

and

1900 Frost Road, Suite 101
Bristol, PA 19007, USA

First Published 1996

A catalogue record of this book is available from the British Library

ISBN 0 335 19401 X (hb)   0 335 19400 1 (pb)

Library of Congress Cataloging-in-Publication Data
McKeganey, Neil P.
    Sex work on the streets: prostitutes and their clients / Neil McKeganey and Marina Barnard.
        p.   cm.
    Includes bibliographical references and index.
    ISBN 0-335-19401-X (hb.). — ISBN 0-335-19400-1 (pbk.)
    1. Prostitutes—Scotland—Glasgow—Attitudes. 2. Prostitution—Scotland—Glasgow. I. Barnard, Marina, 1960–   . II. Title.
HQ187.G58M35   1996
306.74'09414'43—dc20   95-51048
                                                                  CIP

Typeset by Type Study, Scarborough
Printed in Great Britain by Biddles Limited, Guildford and Kings Lynn

For a sparkling star and a baby angel
Rebecca and Gabriel

Maria Magdalena

When I'm there on the street, dressed for work,
up for hire,
It's not me. When I'm there, I'm not there,
Just the bones, just the tits, just the bum,
And the legs, up to here, legs for hire,
I'm not there, it's not me, I'm not there.
Red rouge and mascara,
Lipstick and eyeliner,
Legs to here, lace to here, skirt to here:
In the dark, on the street, what you want,
what you see, what YOU PAY FOR —
It's not me.

The lust that you bring me,
The thrill that you buy,
The sadness that you pay for,
The dirt that you pay for,
The ghost that you long for —
The ghost that you lay —
Is not me. I'm not there
When I'm there on the street, dressed for work,
up for hire,
It's not me . . . I'm not there . . . it's not me.

Sue Glover

Contents

List of tables
and figures

Foreword

Good info

Prostitution is a world-wide phenomenon that has existed for as long as writing itself. One of the earliest codes of law, inscribed on clay tablets in Sumer some 3500 years ago, made the distinction between prostitutes who could not veil themselves, and chaste women, who had to do so. Societies' tolerance or acceptance of prostitution has varied at different times and places, although in no place and at no time has it been entirely without stigma or repression. Today, some or all aspects of prostitution are illegal in all countries, although the approach varies from complete prohibition of every aspect, as in the United States,[1] to the system in place in much of Europe, where, although prostitution itself is not illegal, most aspects related to it are illegal and prostitutes are regularly arrested for 'soliciting', or loitering. In some countries, including Austria, Senegal, Singapore, and Peru, the licensing of prostitution is allied to mandatory health checks backed up by the threat of arrest. A few countries have explored other approaches, including the Netherlands, where both soliciting and engaging in prostitution are legal within specified zones without mandatory licensing and testing, and where prostitution is tolerated outside those zones, so long as the women are discreet. In Australia, the Australian Capital Territory has decriminalized prostitution and a number of other state governments have been looking at a variety of alternatives to criminal law.

From my vantage point in the United States, it was enlightening to read this book because it underscores the fact that even with the less comprehensive prohibition that exists in Glasgow, the workers on the street are subjected to the same harassment as in my country. Indeed, I bring up this legal context because it is the context within which sex workers work, a context that increases their vulnerability to both sexually transmitted diseases (including HIV infection) as discussed in Chapter 5, for which they are so often scapegoated, and violence, described so well in Chapter 6. It is also the context within which many street workers suffer from depression, as documented by a number of researchers,[2] and attempt suicide more often than either the general population of women or off-street prostitutes.[3] In addition, perhaps because of the confluence of criminal laws prohibiting both prostitution and drug use, there is a strong, historical association between the use of drugs and working on the street. It is difficult to know whether women begin prostituting to pay for drugs or begin to use drugs as a way of dealing with the stress of working in this illegal market; both paths are described by the women whose words make up the tapestry of this book. In the end, however, what is amazing is that despite all this, in virtually all countries, sex workers are strong, courageous women, attempting in any way possible to establish control over their work and their lives. In reading this book, I was struck by how clearly the women described their methods of establishing their control of the situation in the first negotiations with the client, and the importance of new workers being trained by those with long experience, as described in Chapter 2.

Perhaps because most societies define the prostitute as a 'criminal', many people care little about either the violence that is committed against prostitutes[4] or the corruption that is often associated with the enforcement of prostitution laws. In many countries, the police exert control over the women who work by extorting money and sex in exchange for not arresting them, and sometimes arrest them anyway. When I was in Manila recently, women working in a massage parlour told me that as many as 15 policemen came by every week to take payment in sex and money. Prostitutes in New York City and San Francisco talk about similar abuses of power.

This general societal blindness has also meant that for most of history, few countries have established social and/or health services designed to meet sex workers' needs, or even to treat them as ordinary human beings. From the prostitutes' side, the centuries of persecution in the name of public health, morality, or public order,[5] have made them wary of both police and health care systems. This manifests itself both in a cautiousness to report those who commit crimes against them to police, described so well in this book, or informing health care providers about their work. This is not the first book to show this, as both individual sex workers and sex workers' rights organizations, and other writers, have discussed these issues in the past.[6] However, this may be the first book to focus on the lives of women working in the UK since the arrival of AIDS.[7]

One would not think there was anything positive about AIDS, but this disaster has forced governments to pay for research on, and sometimes services for, sex workers. It was not an intended effect, but what has happened in a number of countries is that prostitutes' own organizations, and those agencies that have worked with them, have gone beyond the mechanics of AIDS prevention. In Australia, prostitutes are funded by the government to work on AIDS prevention, and a national coalition (the Scarlet Alliance) has been formed to enable them to work for law reform in each state. In the Netherlands, De Rode Draad, the prostitutes' organization originally funded to work on health issues, developed a range of other projects, again with a focus on law reform. In most German cities, sex workers' organizations also work on both health issues and law reform. In Calcutta, India, an AIDS prevention project helped prostitutes form a cooperative that sells condoms and other useful products at reduced prices, and established a credit union, and is working to develop options for ageing workers. In Thailand, the only project accountable to the workers, Empower, became involved in law reform efforts because of what they observed when they began teaching women the languages of their clients, and even more when they focused on how to work more safely. Prostitutes' organizations have also been active on both AIDS issues and law reform in Brazil, Ecuador, Mexico, and Uruguay, and are just beginning to form in places like Senegal and Nigeria. My own organization, the National Task Force on Prostitution, is a loose coalition of sex workers' rights organizations in several states and provinces in the United States and Canada, some of which have been funded to work on AIDS prevention, particularly for street workers, and some of which work with no funds at all, but all of which work towards law reform.

In addition, AIDS permitted both prostitutes' organizations and supportive public health agencies to open drop-in centres for the workers, where they can come for moral support and tips on working safely, including strategies to prevent or cope with violence. Many local governments have funded 'outreach' projects, with health educators going to the workers where they work, either on foot or with a caravan, or both. The best have hired current or former sex workers to act as the health educators, perhaps only dimly understanding the potential for community organizing. Before AIDS no one bothered, and sex workers were ignored by virtually everyone except the police. The point is, preventing AIDS is much more than simply promoting the use of condoms or alternatives to the specific sexual acts that carry the risk of transmission, or even distributing sterile needles to those who inject drugs. In order for sex workers to be able to protect themselves, they have to be able to control their work, which in turn requires that they be free to control their lives.

Looking at their lives beyond their work, as this book does so movingly in Chapter 7, has rarely been done by outside observers. Although I have listened to many of my friends talk about how to help lovers deal with their work, I think this book is one of the first to describe this process so clearly, and to explode the idea of lover as some stereotype of 'pimp' or 'ponce' or 'procurer', and shows them to be feeling, caring partners, as prostitutes have so often claimed. Far from being forced by their lovers to go out on the street, as some outsiders assume, some women in my country, as in Glasgow, prefer to work as prostitutes (which often involves no prison term beyond overnight) than to have their partners get arrested for real crimes such as burglary, which carry much longer prison terms.

Those of us who are not prostitutes know much more about prostitution than we did before, because of the research being done by people like Neil McKeganey and Marina Barnard. Those of us who are prostitutes have more freedom to speak out on our own behalf, in forums such as the International Conference on AIDS and the Fourth World Conference on Women, in meetings closer to home, and in books.[8] As a result, the discourse about prostitution is beginning to change and the nature of services to prostitutes is beginning to be *for* the sex workers, and no longer a way to protect society from them.

Priscilla Alexander
National Task Force on Prostitution
New York City

Notes

1 A minor exception is in counties in the State of Nevada with less than 200,000 or 250,000 population (depending on the source), where communities have the local option to permit closed brothels in which the women (and there are no male brothels) are tightly controlled, including severe restrictions on their movement and mandatory testing to guarantee the clients a 'clean product', as it were.

2 Alegria, Margarita, Vera, Mildren, Freeman, Daniel H., *et al.*, HIV Infection, Risk Behaviors, and Depressive Symptoms among Puerto Rican Sex Workers, *American Journal of Public Health*, 1994; 84: 2000–2002. Also, John Potterat, Colorado Springs, Colorado, personal communication.

3 Diana Prince, doctoral dissertation.

4 In the United States, there has been a kind of epidemic of serial murders of prostitutes during the past decade, with either 45 or more than 100 women killed in Seattle, Washington (depending on who is speaking), another series in Portland, Oregon, and another in San Diego, California, all on the west coast. Some say the three series are separate, others think they may be the work of one man, possibly a truck driver driving up and down the coast. Just in the last two years, one man confessed to killing 13 women working in one district in New York City, without the police even realizing it until the man, Joel Rifkin, was stopped for a moving violation while driving a truck without a licence plate, and the police officers discovered the body of one of the women in the truck. Another killed 10 women in Chicago, Illinois, and although people in the community told the police they thought it was one killer, the police scoffed until they arrested the killer, who confessed to all 10. Another man was recently convicted of killing 12 women in Riverside, California, another has been arrested for killing six in Miami, Florida. No newspaper or television station has examined why so many women have been murdered in so many places.

5 For example, in my encyclopaedic reading on this subject, I have come across more than 600 laws related to prostitution enacted since the beginning of the common era. Five were concerned in some way with improving working conditions or providing redress in the case of crimes against them. All of the others represented efforts to control the workers.

6 Roberts, Nickie, *The Front Line: Women in the Sex Industry Speak*, London, 1986; McLeod, Eileen, *Women Working: Prostitution Now*, London: Croom Helm, 1982.

7 There have been several important articles, including Morgan-Thomas, Ruth, 'AIDS risks, alcohol, drugs, and the sex industry: a Scottish study', in Plant, Martin (ed.), *AIDS, Drugs and Prostitution*, London: Tavistock/Routledge, 1990; Morgan-Thomas, Ruth 'HIV and the Sex Industry', and Maciver, Netta, 'Developing a service for prostitutes in Glasgow', in Bury, Judy, Morrison, Val, McLachlan, Sheena (eds), *Working with Women & AIDS: Medical, social & counselling issues*, London: Tavistock/Routledge, 1992; Barnard, Marina, 'Working in the dark: researching female prostitution', in Roberts, Helen (ed.), *Women's Health Matters*, London: Routledge, 1992; Butcher, Kate, 'Feminists, Prostitutes and HIV', in Doyal, Lesley, Naidoo, Jennie, Wilton, Tamsin (eds), *AIDS: Setting a Feminist Agenda*, London: Taylor & Francis, 1994.

8 See, for example, Bell, Laurie, *Good Girls/Bad Girls: Feminists and Sex Trade Workers Face to Face*, Seattle: Seal Press, 1987, the proceedings of a conference held in Toronto in 1985, and Pheterson, Gail (ed.), *A Vindication of the Rights of Whores*, Seattle: Seal Press, also, Delacoste, Frederique, and Alexander, Priscilla (eds), *Sex Work: Writings by Women in the Sex Industry*, San Francisco: Cleis Press, 1987, Jordan, Jan, *Working Girls: Women in the New Zealand Sex Industry*, Auckland: Penguin Books, 1991.

Acknowledgements

We would like to acknowledge the co-operation of the women and the men who agreed to be interviewed in our research but who, for obvious reasons, we cannot thank by name. This research was conducted whilst we were employed at the Public Health Research Unit at Glasgow University; we would like to thank Dr Andrew Boddy, the Director of that unit, and Dr Alastair Leyland who provided statistical support to our project. Dr Michael Bloor was a co-grant-holder on the project and helped us in some of the fieldwork. We would like to thank Dr Laurence Gruer from the Greater Glasgow Health Board who arranged for us to be provided with condoms and sterile injecting equipment for distribution to the women. We would like to acknowledge Niall Maclean for pointing us towards Goffman in Chapter 7. Eleanor Gallagher assisted us in some of the clerical tasks associated with our work and for that we are very grateful. We owe a special thanks to Evelyn Crombie who typed the last, and numerous previous drafts, and generally ran the office associated with our research. We are grateful to Carfax Publications for allowing us to reprint material from 'Why do men buy sex and what are their assessments of the HIV related risks when they do?', *AIDS Care*, 6: 289–301. We are grateful to Current Science Limited for allowing us to reprint material from 'Prostitution and HIV: what do we know and where might research be targeted in the future', *AIDS*, 8: 1215–26. We are also grateful to Basil Blackwell Publications for allowing us to reprint material from 'Violence and vulnerability: conditions of work for streetworking prostitutes', *Sociology of Health and Illness*, 15(5): 683–705.

The views expressed in this book are not necessarily those of the Medical Research Council, which funded the project, or of the Scottish Office Home and Health Department, which funds the Centre For Drug Misuse Research.

Introduction

In the minds of many people, sex is something which should never be sold. Society's reaction to a famous actor or pop star being caught buying sex may be no more than mild amusement or speculative interest. For a politician to be caught paying for sex, the realization that their private behaviour falls short of their public morality can be sufficient to end their career. Such reactions might seem odd when one considers that there is not a society in the world where sex is not being traded every day and night of the week and that the stock in trade of most prostitutes' work is not the pop star, actor or cabinet minister but the butcher, the baker and the candlestick maker. Similarly, each of us has probably used sex on occasion in an instrumental way to achieve some desired end, whether to attract, to instil a sense of guilt, to win favour, or whatever. Although such behaviour may not exactly be approved of, it does not draw the stigma or legal penalty attached to trading sex for money. We reserve a special language for those women who put a price on sex: hooker, whore, strumpet, prostitute, and harlot, and in doing so signal the unique status of exchanging sex for money.

Prostitution, like sex in general, is surrounded by myths, one of which is the belief that it always involves someone else; the woman who sells sex is never our mother, our daughter, or our sister but some anonymous other who is infinitely more desperate than those we love. Similarly the man who buys sex is never our father, brother, husband or boyfriend, but another whom we do not know and may not even wish to know. The myth that prostitution only involves anonymous others is sustained by the secrecy which surrounds trading sex for money. Once one lifts that secrecy what one finds in abundance is not the perverse, the extraordinary, or the exotic but the commonplace, the ordinary and the everyday. The women and men who appear in this book have the recognizable faces of the people we know. Their circumstances may be different from our own but they are ordinary people living ordinary lives – the fact of their buying or selling sex is a part of those lives rather than the defining characteristic of them. It is no part of the concern of this book to make moral judgements about those involved in the business of prostitution. Such judgements are often made on the basis of a lack of understanding of the people to whom they are applied. Our interest here is in describing the lived reality of selling and buying sex – an ethnography of prostitution.

This book is based upon over three years' research with working women and their clients. Our work began with the task of assessing the risks of HIV infection associated with female street prostitutes in Glasgow. As this work progressed our concerns moved beyond a focus on HIV to look at the wider experience of prostitution. The women we have contacted are in no way representative of prostitutes as a whole. Street prostitutes are only one part, albeit the most visible part, of an economy which encompasses an enormous variety of women who work through agencies, massage parlours, saunas, flats, hotels, etc. To claim that street prostitutes are representative of prostitution as a whole would make as much sense as claiming that crime fiction is representative of all literature. There is quite simply no such thing as a representative sample of women selling sex. What we have tried to do in our research is contact a broad range of women selling sex on the streets. We have interviewed women who have worked for many years and others who have just begun working, women working to finance a drug habit and others who would never use illicit drugs, women who provide only certain sexual services and women providing a wide variety of sexual services, women who are positive about their work and others who have deep regrets about it.

Similarly, in our work with the clients there was no possibility of contacting a representative sample of men buying sex. So hidden is the world of male clients that we have no way of knowing whether buying sex is something which a small proportion of men do very often or something which a large proportion do occasionally. In our research with the clients we tried to interview a broad sample; we have contacted some men who only buy sex on the streets and others who would never buy sex on the streets, men who always make a point of going to the same woman and men who never return to the same woman twice. Despite such variety we have done little more than gain a glimpse of the world of men who buy sex. This is a glimpse worth taking, however, if for no other reason than the fact that most descriptions of prostitution concentrate solely on the women selling sex rather than the men who buy it.

Despite our focus on street prostitution in Glasgow, many aspects of the experience of the women will undoubtedly resonate with women selling sex in other cities and other locations. Some of the issues confronting prostituting women in particular will find echoes among women more generally. Equally the voices of the male clients we interviewed echo sentiments which many men share. This is not to say that all men have the potential to be clients but it is to emphasize that we should not necessarily view men as deviant simply because they have paid for sex.

The first chapter provides an explanation of how the research which informs this book was conducted in the red-light area in Glasgow. We look at how we set about contacting female prostitutes and male clients and the kinds of relationships we were able to establish with them. The chapter outlines some of the pitfalls of the kind of fieldwork we have been involved in, including the risks of violence which this work entailed. In Chapter 2 we describe the operation of the red-light area and the working patterns of the women. We present some of the quantitative information on the street prostitution scene in Glasgow. This includes the number of women working, their ages, and the kinds of sex they were selling. The second part of the chapter describes the experience of selling sex from the perspective of the women.

In Chapter 3 we describe the enormous impact which injecting drug use had on the street prostitution scene in Glasgow; we look at the extent of drug injecting among the women as well as the way in which their drug use would influence their work. In Chapter 4 we shift our focus from the women selling sex to the men buying sex. We describe the background of the clients, their age and marital status, and the kinds of sex they were buying. The main part of the chapter looks at the men's views and experiences of paid sex. We look at what they saw as the particular appeal of contacting a prostitute, why they were buying sex, their views of prostitute women and their concerns in relation to HIV. We also look at the men's attitudes towards disclosing to their own sexual partners that they have paid for sex.

The belief that prostitute women may be spreading HIV infection to their 'innocent' clients (and to the partners of those clients) has led some commentators to call for the decriminalization of prostitution, and others for the imposition of further legal constraints to stop women working. In Chapter 5 we look at some of the facts, rather than the fictions, to do with HIV and prostitution, and review what is currently known about the extent of HIV infection among prostitute women in different parts of the world. This chapter also contains more detailed information on the extent of HIV among the street working women we interviewed, their attitudes towards HIV and their use of condoms with clients.

Despite the plethora of media attention which has been focused on prostitution as a result of concerns over the spread of HIV, the greatest risk to the health of such women (at least in the developed countries) comes not from a deadly virus but from the violent actions of many of their clients. In Chapter 6 we describe the violence which was an everyday feature of the street prostitution scene. We describe the kinds of violent attacks to which the women were routinely subjected, their responses to such violence and their strategies for minimizing the risk of being attacked. We show how such violence can largely be explained in terms of the perception of prostitute women as being no more than the sex they are selling.

In Chapter 7 we shift the focus from the public to the private to look at the impact of the women's work on their home lives. All of the women we interviewed were at pains to draw a clear distinction between their private, home life and their work life. As we show in this chapter, maintaining that distinction was not always an easy task; it involved a delicate balancing act which was not always successfully sustained, either by the women or by their partners. Finally, in Chapter 8 we conclude the book by looking at the implications of our work in relation to the delivery of services to prostitute women. We also consider some of the arguments for and against changing the legal status of prostitution.

Throughout the book we have included excerpts from our interviews and our field diaries. To maintain the anonymity of the people we have contacted, all names and certain minor biographical details have been altered.

1

Researching prostitutes and their clients

Introduction

The purpose of this chapter is to describe our research methods. We describe the experience of carrying out this work, our perception of the red-light area, and our method of establishing contact with prostitute women. In the course of this chapter we also raise a number of issues to do with buying and selling sex which are more fully discussed in later chapters. Since our research over the last three years has been with the women selling sex we will start with this aspect of our work and then describe our research on male clients.

Researching female prostitutes

In the early days of our research we took a decision which shaped all of our subsequent work, namely to try and contact women directly on the streets. Often other researchers studying prostitution have contacted women in a variety of formal settings and have, for example, interviewed women attending genito-urinary clinics, or attending court proceedings for solicitation. As an alternative we decided to go to those parts of the city where women were working and to approach them directly to see if they would be prepared to be interviewed.

To do this necessitated the creation of an acceptable social role in order to be in the red-light area in the first place. With the agreement of the local health board and having informed the local police of what we intended to do, we adopted a quasi-service-provider role which entailed providing women working on the streets with supplies of condoms, sterile injecting equipment, information on HIV risk reduction and telephone numbers of a variety of local services. Each night's fieldwork within the red-light area consisted of walking round all of the streets where sex was being sold, approaching as many women as possible, introducing ourselves and offering them the various items we were carrying. In this way we gradually became familiar to the women and this in turn facilitated the build-up of sufficiently good relationships with the women to allow the research to proceed. Because our research was concerned in part with identifying the extent of HIV infection among street-based prostitutes, we also needed to ask each of the women we contacted to provide a sample of their saliva, collected using suitable equipment, which could then be tested anonymously for signs of HIV infection.

In total we carried out more than 800 hours of fieldwork in the main red-light areas in Glasgow spread over a three-year period. We carried out our work from the sunniest days in Glasgow to near blizzard conditions (when sex would still be being traded), from midday to 2 a.m. or 3 a.m.

The red-light area

It is difficult to convey the quality of the red-light area other than to say it was a world of extremes in which it frequently seemed as if anything might happen next and it very often did. One moment the streets would be empty, the next they would be teeming with cars; in one street a woman would be emerging from an alleyway with a client, in another a drug dealer might be being wrestled to the floor by undercover police. Other nights the streets would be quiet for hours on end. At times our fieldwork felt a bit like watching a series of overlapping films in which one had only the slimmest understanding of plot and person:

> Our arrival in the area tonight coincided with an increase in police activity. We had seen a police van hurtling down the street as we entered the red-light area. Marina wanted to go and have a look down the street it had turned into when suddenly the van appeared behind us hammering up the street, siren wailing as it came up behind a red Ford Escort which immediately pulled over – two uniformed police jumped out of the van and began searching the driver. Meanwhile a guy in a bomber jacket and jeans [police] ran past us and joined in the search. The two occupants of the car were led away into the police van. When later we saw the guy in bomber jacket and jeans talking to the two policemen, he looked well satisfied.

In the early days of our fieldwork, the unpredictability of the area created a sense of tension on our part. From time to time we would be approached by men who were hanging round the area, whose motives were unclear, and whose presence would increase our anxiety:

> Marina and I had just given a set of needles and syringes to a woman when she called us over and asked if she could have a set for her man. Although we do operate a tacit policy of providing only to the women, we both felt it would be better on this occasion to give the guy a set. As Marina fished into the bag for a set I kept my eye on the guy whom I could see was trying to

get a sight of what was in the bag. This made me feel distinctly uncomfortable and I was relieved when we moved off. However fifteen minutes or so later the guy called out to us and started asking about the needles and syringes and seemed very interested in them. He also said that there was a group of women a couple of streets away to whom we could give them. I said we would catch up with them. He then asked if we were walking along the road and said that he would walk with us. We moved off as a group of three and I inserted myself between Marina and he. I became aware as we walked along of someone behind us. Somehow I felt it unwise to move off the main street so I stopped, let the guy behind us walk past and then made it clear that we had no intention of continuing to walk with the guy . . . I had a very definite sense that the guy might have intended taking the bag although equally, of course, the whole thing might have been innocent.

Our concerns over such incidents arose not from any explicit threat, but from our own uncertainty as to what might or might not happen in the area. There was a noticeable reduction in our anxiety once we became more familiar with the area and more confident in our ability to distinguish between situations of real and imagined threat.

Whether we were right to feel more confident in our ability to judge what was happening within the area is difficult to say. Violence involving the women, their clients, and sundry others was an ever present feature of the area. Indeed, as we describe in Chapter 6, there was hardly a night in our fieldwork when at least one of the women was not bearing the signs of some kind of recent assault. In a way our own situation mirrored that of the women; both we and they had to avoid becoming so anxious about the possibility of violence as to make it impossible to carry on working, while at the same time not becoming so blasé about the dangers as to take unnecessary risks. This balance had to be struck without ever really knowing the actual level of threat involved.

It was an amusing, ironic aspect of our fieldwork that the only occasion we were involved in anything approximating a physical confrontation involved not the people whom we had been most concerned with, but the police:

Marina and I were standing chatting to one woman to whom we had just given condoms and injecting equipment. Out of the corner of my eye I caught sight of two guys moving towards us really quickly. As I turned to face them, one of them pushed me back forcefully against the wall. I could see his police warrant card as I was pinned back. He asked if I had anything in my pockets but before I could answer he had taken out my notebook and flipped through the pages. I said that he was making a mistake and asked if we had to run through this in the street. I explained who we were and said that we had ID. He, realizing that I was not dealing drugs, relaxed his grip. I could see the other guy standing with Marina speaking into his radio. The two police then spoke briefly to each other, he then offered his apologies and said it would be better if all the police knew what we were doing. I said that it was in order to avoid such incidents that we let the local police know each time we started fieldwork. Afterwards Marina explained that the second guy had been much less heavy-handed. She had been able to show him her ID and he had commented to Marina that his partner always jumps in with two feet!

It would be wrong to present our fieldwork as an unbroken period of concern for our own safety and that of the women; there were also moments of hilarity which in their own way were as much a part of the red-light area as the atmosphere of potential violence. Some of the moments of greatest humour involved witnessing how the women managed their contacts with clients:

We were chatting with Sandy [a prostitute in her mid 50s] when a guy in his 20s approached and stood next to Sandy with a kind of pleading look on his face. After a few moments of all of us ignoring him he tried to interject himself into our conversation. Sandy at this point turned to him and flatly asked him to stand to one side before resuming her conversation with us. She explained to us that they had been in an alley when the police drove through. Both she and the client had shot off, the latter before reaching a climax. According to Sandy he was now waiting to be finished off. As Sandy explained this, the client edged back towards us, she disdainfully dispatched him with a cursory 'I'm getting some rubbers, you stand over there'. At one point he went down the way rather than in the direction Sandy had indicated and she caught this out of the corner of her eye; 'Not there I said, up there,' she said in a haughty voice. To my amazement he meekly followed her directions. When he moved off just out of earshot, Sandy looked skywards and in a sing-song voice said, 'There's nae fuckin' way you're gettin' me again tonight so you can get tae fuck little boy.'

Contacting the women

How to approach the women? What to say? How would they react? Would there be pimps in the area and if so what would they make of what we were trying to do? These were just some of the questions which characterized the first days of our work. As is often the case, most of these uncertainties receded once the work began in earnest. As it turned out, it was surprisingly easy to contact the women and although there were some individuals who remained wary of us, we did manage with time, and through our continued presence in the area, to build up good working relationships with many of the women. It helped enormously that we always worked in a pair thereby boosting each other's enthusiasm on the occasions when it waned.

In the course of our work we contacted over 300 women. The time spent with the women and the kinds of things talked about were largely determined by them. On occasion our contacts with the women would amount to no more than a nod of recognition or a fleeting few sentences. The same woman who might one night spend a long time talking might, the next, cut short any such contact. If a woman was busy or if she felt that we were interrupting her business, contact would be brief:

> We met up with Iona, an injecting drug user. I've known her on and off for about three years now but this time she looked the worse for wear. Usually our contacts have been very friendly. However this time it was clear she didn't want to talk since she very quickly said, 'Look, no' bein' cheeky or nothin' I've got to work. I've been down here hours and I've only got 20 quid [pounds] to show for it.'

> After a quiet night we saw Gillian whom we'd kept missing the night before and wanted to talk to. As we approached her, she, barely turning, said, 'I've got a punter,' and that was her, gone. She later said she'd been afraid we'd put off the client and lose her business because we look like the vice [police].

Such encounters were salutary reminders both of the fact that the women's reasons for being in the area were solely to earn money and, relatedly of the marginal status we had in so far as the women were concerned. At other times when business was very quiet we would often stand chatting with the women at length. Such conversations most often centred around aspects of the women's work although not exclusively so:

> We met up with Sally and Eileen, both of whom we have seen on many occasions previously. They were sitting together on a low wall, chatting. It's incredibly quiet tonight and nearly all of the women have commented how slow business is. We sat with them for a while. I asked them about using condoms for oral sex and Sally cupped two hands to her lips and imitated giving oral sex stressing that only the very tip of the penis touched her lips. She winked 'prostitutes' trick of the trade that is'. She then went on to evidence how little contact she has with a client in the cars since she makes sure she sits with her backside off the back of the seat so she can get her hands round and instead of having sex inside her the man is really having sex into her hand cupped into a hole, 'Best thing ever invented that baby oil, they cannae tell a thing, they're moaning away and saying how tight you are and all the time they're screwing your hands.' Eileen who was listening throughout this commented that her job as a prostitute was a combination of actor, counsellor, doctor and nurse.

Although there were some women with whom we had very good relationships, there were others who over the course of the three years of our work were assiduous at keeping their distance from us:

> One woman whom we approached tonight politely but firmly told us she wanted nothing to do with any agency or anything else. She also chose not to use the prostitute drop-in, she would rather buy her own condoms, not take free ones. 'I don't need anybody lookin' into ma business. I know what I do and it's ma private life, naebody else's.'

Over time within the area, we were able to gradually chip away at some of the more negative reactions from some women and establish, if not a warm and friendly relationship, at least a tolerance of our presence in the area:

A quiet night out although we did manage to meet up with a woman we'd not spoken to before. We also met Amanda. Neil didn't think she'd have anything to do with us so he went on to talk to Elise. Amanda has a rather off-putting manner, she can be very intimidating. I asked her if she wanted condoms, she said she had them coming out of her ears and anyway there weren't any punters but lots of police. Feeling pleased that I'd not been immediately knocked back, I then asked her if she'd agree to do the HIV saliva test. I explained about confidentiality and anonymity etc. and surprisingly enough she agreed to do it. Taking the cotton swab from me she put it between her teeth, warning that she had 'falsies' [false teeth]. Just as I was silently congratulating myself she pulled it out saying 'Oh no, it tastes horrid, I'm no' doin' that!'

Working on the streets in daily contact with the women provided us with a unique insight into their work. At times we saw women carrying out their work of attracting clients with a deftness that left us virtually speechless. At other times we were left with an acute sense of the desperation and vulnerability of some women:

Anita [a drug injector] was standing in a lot of pain from one of two abscesses on her back that had still to be lanced. It was an enormous swelling. She said she felt dizzy and sick and cold but she had to earn the money she needs. She can't do sex at the moment because of her back so all she does is oral and hand jobs.

Stood chatting briefly to Eileen who looked cold and vulnerable leaning alone against one of the buildings; as we approached she waved at a passing car and then disconsolately turned to us: 'That's one of ma regulars and he just ignored me'. I commented that maybe he hadn't seen her – no she said he had driven round four times and ignored her each time.

One particularly distressing occasion concerned coming across a woman whom one of us (MB) had originally interviewed at a residential drug detoxification unit about two years previously. We knew she was prostituting because we had met her in the area the previous year:

As ever she was nervous and highly strung. She begged me to get her some clothes saying she'd nothing, that all she was wearing was borrowed from a pal. She said she didn't even have underwear. I asked her where her stuff was and from her answer it was either stolen or she sold it. Anyway, she then pulled me to one side and whispered that she'd been diagnosed as HIV positive. This came as a surprise because although her ex-boyfriend was HIV positive I knew she'd been tested two or three times and each time it was a negative result. Her revelation made me feel acutely how very troubled her life had been and how impotent I was. I told her I'd try and get some clothes to her at the Salvation Army hostel (where she was staying) at which she burst into tears. The whole situation was extremely distressing.

Interviewing and observation

In many areas of sociological research one is reliant upon what people say about their behaviour rather than what can be observed (Vangelder and Kaplan, 1992). In the case of our own research, for example, we needed to collect information on the extent to which condoms were used by prostitutes and their clients. Clearly it was never going to be possible to actually observe sexual liaisons between client and prostitute and as a result much of the information we have on this topic arises from the interviews conducted with women and male clients. By carrying out fieldwork within the red-light area, however, it was sometimes possible to observe the negotiations between prostitutes and their clients and to see whether the issue of condoms featured within such negotiations:

> I was standing with a woman getting condoms and injecting equipment from my bag when a man passed slowly by. Seeing this the woman turned to face him and asked if he was looking for business. He didn't appear to speak much English but nodded that he was – the woman continued 'Aye well it's £10 in the motor and £25 in a flat'. He said that he didn't have a car, to which she replied, 'It'll have to be in the lane then.' He then asked with or without Durex. Initially the woman did not understand what he had said but then responded, 'Och no it'll have to be with a Durex unless you wank yourself off and I'll let you have a feel of me for £15.' To this he added, 'I want to fuck but I don't like Durex.' She said, 'Well you've got to have one if you fuck, if you'll no' wear a Durex I'm no' doin' any business with you, none of the lassies down here will, you should mind that by the way.'

Our fieldwork contacts with the women were a valuable source of information. However, as might be expected, there were limits to what could be understood through such contact. For reasons of personal safety we confined our work within the red-light area to the main street where women would stand waiting to contact clients. We deliberately did not enter the warren of alleyways leading off the main streets where women would frequently take clients to provide them with sex. This decision inevitably limited our understanding of the area and of the nature of trading sex. That this was the case was forcefully brought to our attention on the one occasion when we did walk down one of the alleys:

> Ordinarily we keep to the main streets and avoid the alleys. This evening we took a short cut down one of the alleys, 20 or so yards into the alley I saw some movement off to one side. As we got closer I could make out a woman on her knees giving a client oral sex. The whole thing looked incredibly mechanical. Marina and I retreated back down the alley. We have been speaking to the women for many months now, such that their talk about their work has become almost commonplace. This was the first occasion that the reality of what being a prostitute entails has been made starkly apparent – alone, on your knees, with a client's penis in your mouth. It is difficult to say why but it was incredibly shocking to see that

reality. It also brought home just how vulnerable the women are with a client standing over them.

By suddenly being able to witness the actual provision of paid sex we realized how much of our contact with the women consisted of them talking about their work. The routinized manner in which relations with clients tended to be discussed did in a sense belie the actual reality of the nature of the work they were doing once they entered a client's car or walked down an alleyway with a client.

Setting limits to our relationships with the women

By working as a couple we felt that the possibility of the women and the clients misinterpreting our presence within the red-light area was reduced (although it did mean that we were on occasions mistaken for police by some women). There were nevertheless times when we were asked to do things or offered services which were incompatible with the role we had adopted:

> This evening we met MJ [drug injector] who seemed in a pretty agitated state walking up and down the same bit of the street looking intently into the passing cars. She immediately approached us and said that she hadn't done any business that night, she was desperate for money and couldn't even buy a packet of fags. The latter followed up with a request for us to buy her a packet. We said that we couldn't [we'd made a decision earlier on not to get into the business of providing cigarettes since it can so easily get out of hand]. We were firm, which irritated her. Then we rounded the corner at which point she veered off because she saw a man walking along. Alice [another prostitute] was also apparently in pursuit of him although in fact he didn't appear to be looking for business. MJ paid no mind to Alice and cut across the road to ask him if he wanted business. Halfway down the road she again caught up with us, this time shouting to us to stop a white car waiting to drive across the intersecting road. I couldn't catch what she said and asked her to repeat it, in total three times. This irritated MJ still further who said as she ran past in pursuit of the white car, 'I asked you three times.' There hardly seemed any point in explaining to her that it was not part of our work to attract clients for the women. All night long she was chasing business, stopping any man who happened to be in the area and almost flinging herself in cars as they drove by.

On another occasion one of the women sought medical advice from McKeganey on the treatment of a possible abscess:

> Tessa approached and asked if she could have a word in private with me, so we walked round the corner – she said that she thought she had an abscess on her breast and would I have a look at it. Before I could answer she was pulling down her top and lifting up her breast. I said that it was not necessary for me to look at it and that it would be better for her to go along to the drop-in clinic and speak to the doctor there. Tessa said she still had antibiotics from a previous abscess which she could use. I explained that it

would be better to speak to the doctor first. Throughout this, cars were passing by and there was not the slightest question of embarrassment, on Tessa's part it was as if they simply did not exist; however she had not wanted to raise the possibility of an abscess in front of Marina – odd really.

Working in the red-light area over an extended period of time enabled us to build up fairly close research relationships with many of the women. While such relationships proved valuable in our research, they also constrained our work in ways of which we were not always fully aware. We began to wonder if the kind of relationships we were establishing with the women, and the fact that those relationships occurred within the red-light area itself, might be influencing the kind of information we were getting from the women. For example, we routinely asked women about their use of condoms with clients, only to be provided with the unanimous response that condoms were always used. It seemed likely to us that despite such claims there must have been occasions when condoms were not used and certainly many of the women we spoke to alleged that there were women working in the area who were not using condoms. A small number of women also described occasions when, through violence or whatever, a client had refused to wear a condom:

> The first woman we spoke to this evening described how on the previous evening she had been picked up by a punter, had been taken by him to do business when a man who had been hiding in the car boot appeared. They had both raped her, stolen her money and her leather jacket. Unprompted by us she said they had not used a condom 'so I'm gonnae have to go for an AIDS test'.

We wondered whether the fact of there being a strong occupational culture among the women (such that it was unacceptable for a woman to admit to not having used a condom with a client) might be stopping some women from describing those occasions when condoms had not been used. To try and dilute the possible influence of that shared culture we carried out a small survey of 68 women. By using an explicit research prop – the questionnaire – and explaining to the women that it would take 15 to 20 minutes to complete, and would require taking time out from work, we tried to get information on those possible occasions when for one reason or another a woman might not have been able to use a condom with her client. Once again however we were provided with reports of universal condom use with clients. Our second strategy was to interview 20 women at length in their own home. These interviews were of enormous value not only in allowing us to discuss the nature of the women's work in a more relaxed setting but also in allowing us to see the women in their own homes, in their roles as mothers, girlfriends etc. We were also able to ask the women to describe those occasions when their contact with clients had developed in ways other than they had intended. In doing so we were provided with detailed descriptions of the violence which many of the women had been subjected to in their work during which there had indeed been occasions when condoms had not been used.

The nature of our fieldwork also raised certain ethical dilemmas (Barnard 1992; McKeganey *et al.* 1994). We have already outlined the fact that we were providing women with, among other things, sterile injecting equipment. Combining the role of researcher and outreach service provider in this way was problematic on more than one occasion:

> We saw Netta, as usual with Greta, who is much older than her but likes a drink as much as Netta does. From something that Netta let slip, I'm fairly certain that she is only 14 years old but has over the past few months become more and more a part of the life of the area. She does prostitute but only intermittently. Tonight she said she was earning her money for some drink. As we left her she asked us if we had any needles. I said, no, I wasn't going to give her any, she'd have to get them from the drop-in centre. To this she answered, with some justification, 'How come you gie them out to every cunt but me?' This is the uncomfortable decision Neil and I have arrived at on the basis of her age and the fact that she appears only to be experimenting with injecting. If she gets needles from them then at least they can counsel her properly. All the same we are acutely aware that such a decision could have negative ramifications if she then felt obliged to share. We are still so uncertain as to the right way to proceed on this one.

By providing this young girl with sterile injecting equipment we might have been guilty of encouraging her to inject; however, in refusing to do so we might equally have been increasing her chances of needing to share needles and syringes with other people and placing her at increased risk of HIV as a result. There are no guidelines covering what we should have done on such occasions and as a result we acted in the way which seemed most appropriate to ourselves at the time.

Researching male clients

The difficulties we anticipated in the early days of our research contacting female prostitutes were nothing compared to the difficulties we faced in contacting the clients. As with our work with the women, we intended to contact men directly in the red-light area, this we felt was at least one way of getting round the problem of men concealing the fact of their having paid for sex. While it was relatively easy to identify men repeatedly returning to the red-light area to contact women selling sex, most of the men we approached declined to be interviewed or provided a plainly spurious reason for being in the area. At times our approach would be very low key ('This is an area used by working women and I was wondering if you had been approached?') at other times more direct ('I'm carrying out a study of men who have paid for sex – would you mind being interviewed?'). Whichever version we used, the response was almost always the same, a more or less polite 'get lost'. There were, though, some notable successes which were frequent enough to persuade us that it was worth continuing with the fieldwork without being so numerous as to be sufficient for our study:

> This afternoon Mick and I interviewed our first client. I wouldn't feel any better if I'd won the pools. We approached the guy in his car and said that

we were carrying out a confidential study of men who might have had contact with women injecting drugs. He agreed to be interviewed but then in response to our first question about paying for sex, said that he had never done that – both Mick and I were pretty certain we'd seen him on numerous previous occasions in the area picking up women but we decided to leave it at that. An hour or so later, as we were just about to finish the afternoon's fieldwork, a car pulled up alongside us and the same guy said that he had not been honest in response to our earlier questions and that he had paid for sex. I asked him if he would be prepared to be interviewed about those contacts and he said he would – we then sat in his car and ran through our interview schedule about past prostitute contacts, current partners etc.

Even when we were able to interview a client, the interview itself would have an edgy quality arising in large part from our anxiety that after having worked so long and hard at getting the interview, we did not want to frighten them off by being too direct in our questioning:

Second client today and we are now beginning to recognize clients' cars by sight, having seen them repeatedly now cruising the area. Almost immediately I spotted the white Mercedes that I had seen on a number of occasions. When the driver pulled up some 20 or so yards in front of us we decided to try for an interview – by the time we had located our questionnaire, pens etc. he was off. Ten or so minutes later he was back and this time we were quicker off the mark. As we approached the car I could see he was a big guy almost too big for the car – and it was a big car. I explained who we were and what we were doing and asked if he would mind being interviewed – he sort of nodded in a way that I was not sure amounted to a yes but decided to proceed anyway to the first question, 'Have you had any health problems lately?' At this point he looked up and I immediately thought he was going to tell us to 'f. off'. I mumbled something to the effect that the research was anonymous and no big deal when he said, 'Hasn't everybody?' I continued with the questionnaire, though it felt a bit ridiculous doing this standing by the side of the car.

To supplement the meagre total of nine street interviews we asked staff in the local genito-urinary clinics if they would routinely ask men attending for appointments whether they had had recent contact with a female prostitute. Through this means we were able to obtain information from a further 68 men.

The major boost in our efforts at contacting men who had paid for sex came as a result of an advertisement we placed in a tabloid newspaper. This asked men who had recently paid for sex to ring us on a specific number. From early morning on the day our advert appeared, the phone hardly stopped ringing, enabling us to interview a further 66 clients. With the cloak of anonymity which the telephone provided, the men's reticence at talking about having paid for sex disappeared and it was possible to ask them not only straight-forward factual information about the number of women they had bought sex from and the kind of sex purchased, but also the more sensitive areas of what attracted them to paid sex, what they looked for in a prostitute, and their concerns in relation to HIV.

Conclusion

Looking back on this period of field research it is apparent that a good deal of what was achieved was arrived at through a process of trial and error. There was no blueprint for us to follow and no one to smooth our entrance into this different world. The mix of research methods we used was largely a response to the particularities of gathering information in the context of street prostitution. As in all things there were disadvantages as well as advantages for each method used. Similarly each research problem solved would raise different issues for us to grapple with. So, for example, the incorporation of a service provider role provided us with a means of sustained contact with the women. In turn this had ramifications for the way in which the women perceived us and consequently had some influence on the kinds of information provided. So, too, the provision of needles and syringes was not unproblematic in that it raised ethical issues concerning the provision of means to inject illegal drugs, an issue which was particularly present in the case of the 14-year-old girl asking us for needles. Our responses to such issues were based on a pragmatic reasoning of how best to serve the interests of the research while not undermining those of the women researched. Sometimes we got it right, other times we had to think again. Over time we achieved a more sure-footed familiarity with the world we were researching; we knew many of the women and understood something of the culture of the area. There were never any illusions though. We were privileged in being able to glimpse their world, but knew we were never more than bystanders at its very margins.

2

Selling sex: the views
of the women

Introduction

In this chapter we consider the process by which sex is sold and the way in which this is experienced by the women. The first part of the chapter describes streetworking prostitution as it occurs in Glasgow, including the physical characteristics of the area, the number of women working, their relationships with each other, their reasons for starting and stopping working and their relationships with the police. In the second part of the chapter we concentrate more on the experience of selling sex and describe the kind of sex being sold, and the women's negotiations with clients.

The Glasgow red-light district

There are two distinct parts of the city where women work from the street to attract clients. One of these operates during the daytime to the east of the city. It is both small and clandestine as a result of concerted opposition by local residents and businesses, and vigorous policing to control it. Prostitution in this area tends therefore to be a rather low key affair, with women being dressed in their everyday clothes to avoid attracting police attention. Although we did carry out research in this area, it is the red-light area in the centre of town which forms the main focus of this study. The night-time prostitution scene is different altogether. It takes place in the centre of Glasgow's business district, an area full of offices and little else. As the offices empty at night so the streets gradually fill out with women beginning their night's work as prostitutes.

The area itself comprises about eight streets on a grid-like pattern. In turn these streets are bisected by alleyways. As the area is predominantly set up to serve a daytime population of office workers, there are few amenities open in

at night. If a woman is known to prostitute she is often not welcome
w bars open in the area. There are, however, two facilities provided
ecifically for the women, a prostitute drop-in centre (which provides
gynaecological services and a needle exchange for women involved in drug
injecting as well as being a venue for women to take a break from working on
the streets) and a Christian City Mission. The emphasis of this latter group is
on providing for the material, physical and spiritual well-being of the women
they come into contact with.

Women who are prostituting in the area tend to stand on street corners,
either in ones or twos. Occasionally there are larger groups but these are
generally temporary and in between bouts of work. The stereotypical picture
of the streetworking prostitute's attire (low top, short skirt, stilettos) is
sometimes in evidence but it is clear that there is no one way to dress. Some
women do consciously dress provocatively, others choose to dress neatly, still
others make no apparent effort at all.

Although the area at night is predominantly peopled by women selling sex
and men looking to buy it, there are also other interested parties in the area.
The red-light district exerts a magnetism for some people whose interest is
perhaps best described as voyeuristic. So there are often carloads of people
who come to look and perhaps also to shout (mostly pejorative) comments at
the women. Then there are those who are aware of the earning potential of
prostitution and may seek to capitalize on this, either by selling certain items
to the women or, in some cases, to prey on them. It was often the case that
women were offered drugs by people who came specifically to the area to sell
them. As for robberies and extortion, there was evidence that this was a
regular hazard of earning relatively large sums of money and having only
limited places to keep that money safely. Women reported being mugged by
clients (although it should be said that clients similarly reported being
mugged by some prostitutes). We describe the violence which was very much
a part of the red-light area in Chapter 6.

Other interested parties liable to be in the area are boyfriends and husbands
of the prostitutes. Often women would describe their partner's presence in
the area as being to offer guardianship and so reduce the chances of danger
from clients. They would also often take the money as it was earned to reduce
the potential for a woman to be mugged and lose the money. Perhaps these
men would be classed as pimps; however, the women did not regard them as
such and certainly their descriptions of their relationships with partners do
not accord easily with descriptions of pimps that have come from women
working in other British cities and further afield, for example in the United
States.

The presence of so many different parties whose interests do not necessarily run in the same direction means that the area possesses a certain
volatility. The police task of regulating prostitution in accordance with the
laws on soliciting involves also trying to keep a check on the various tensions
which erupt from time to time. One measure has been to actively discourage
the partners of prostitutes from staying in the area with certain penalties
being imposed on both the woman and her partner if the man remains in the
area. This does appear to have reduced some of the tensions liable to erupt,

particularly since it was often the case that many of these men were also involved in the sale of drugs to other women:

> While talking to a woman, a guy, whom she appeared to know, came over. He said he was 'punting 'gesics' [selling Temgesics]. She said she'd already been asked to try and sell some of her pal Spider's eggs [temazepam] so she didn't need any more. He then left, asking her to pass the message on.

Police responses to prostitution and its regulation differ substantially from city to city as much as from country to country. Edinburgh street prostitutes report heavy policing, a factor which perhaps partially explains the relatively small size of the street population there. London prostitutes similarly report vigorous policing in an effort to suppress it or drive it from particular areas, as in Soho. In Glasgow the police response to street prostitution for the most part appears to be one of controlling it rather than attempting its suppression. The style of policing in the city centre red-light area is for example very different to the way in which it is dealt with in the more residential area to the east of the city. Here the police are actively involved in its suppression and do not tolerate its presence, as evidenced by their vigilance in charging any woman thought to be soliciting in the area. In the city centre by contrast there appears evidence of what could be described as a rota system with women being charged with soliciting on a regular basis over a length of time. Women were often heard to say that it was coming up to their turn for being charged and so also being fined in the courts:

> See if you're all right wi' them [the police], they're all right wi' you, that's what I notice and like if you've had the jail [shorthand for being fined] in the past couple of weeks ye'll get it the next couple of weeks, ye know what I mean, they'll gie ye a certain time, a run, four to five weeks.

It often appeared from the way the women talked about the police, and also on the basis of observation, that police and prostitutes had reached a certain accommodation with each other, dependent upon a recognition of where the limits lay. Much the most important of these limits related to the police's setting of the boundaries of where it was and was not permissible for the women to work. Women who transgressed these perimeters knew they would undoubtedly be charged if caught. There were supposedly other criteria used to judge whether or not a woman stood a greater likelihood of being charged; these, however, seemed more arbitrary, and may to an extent have been mythologized. Women reported that police would accept a woman working if she was working safely, if she had condoms or was not undercharging for example, or if she was not too obviously under the influence of drugs:

> At the end of the last evening worked we'd just finished talking to a woman when she was approached by the police and booked for soliciting. We talked about this with Audrey who said she'd been picked up because she was 'full o' it. It was too obvious, that's how she got picked up.'

Whatever the truth of these assertions it was clear that women for the most part thought there were certain conventions which if adhered to would reduce the chances of them being charged by police. Some women referred to giving uniformed police 'the courtesy of the road' by walking (or even by just looking) in the opposite direction from them. This was not a tactic to avoid possible arrest since uniformed police (at least at the time of this study) were not directly involved in the regulation of prostitution; this was the domain of the street offences' unit which had responsibility for this area. An understanding of this 'rule' is demonstrated in one woman's irritated refusal to accept it:

At one point when we were speaking to a woman the police pulled alongside on the other side of the road. She turned to her friend, 'They expect us to move along the road, show them the courtesy of the road, well, I'm no' movin'. I wantae get right up their noses, fuckin' bastards, animals they are.' A little while longer and she did however move.

Given that sex is sold from saunas and massage parlours, from hotels and also from the homes of those women who advertise their services, it may seem strange that sex should be sold from the street at all. Compared to settings such as saunas, street work may seem more arduous as it involves standing outside in all kinds of weather for long or short periods of time depending on how long it takes to get the next client. Having attracted a client the streetworking woman has the increased hazard of going away to a place where sex can be provided in relative privacy. Often this will entail being in deserted car parks or ill-lit streets. In the saunas, on the other hand, the scope for the client to act aggressively or refuse to pay or use a condom is negligible, particularly as sauna managers are likely to be in close proximity to the women working there. However, so far as street women are concerned, there are tangible benefits to be had from this kind of work. When asked why they did so, many women cited the flexibility in being able to decide when to work and for how long. Shift work, which is the norm in saunas and massage parlours, was viewed negatively, particularly where women had children and claimed they could not be sure of adequate childcare arrangements during the daytime. Another point made by those women who had tried working in the saunas related to the numbers of men using the service; women spoke of long periods of time spent doing nothing because of a lack of trade. On the streets in a similar situation women can leave the area and go and do something else. Streetworking women referred to the advantages of being their own boss: in particular they, unlike women working in the saunas, did not have to pay the sauna manager a fee or a percentage of their takings.

These were the kinds of reasons women provided for preferring to work from the streets, even while recognizing the greater relative comfort and safety of working in a more structured environment. Another factor which played an important part in determining the use of street as opposed to other kinds of prostitution related to injecting drug use. Women who used drugs intravenously knew that they would lose their place at the saunas or massage parlours if discovered:

Sarah had worked in the saunas before coming onto the streets. She felt that things had changed because of AIDS: 'They check your arms, kinda thing, you know what I mean. I always, as I say, have a couple of pills and I don't have to hit up smack to get a buzz out of it. So my arms can be clean. But there have been times when I have been hittin' up and when I've been in they've no' given me a check and they've no' tippled [realized she's a drug injector]. I just always wear long sleeves and use the dimmer switch if I've got track marks, I just put the light down.'

Furthermore the requirement that a woman regularly works for set periods of time in such establishments did run counter to the exigencies imposed by addiction in that the necessity to service the drug habit could, and often did, result in a rather chaotic lifestyle.

This is not to say that there was no overlap between streetworking prostitution and other types of prostitution. There were women who worked the streets who had also worked in the saunas and some who had worked through placing advertisements in certain newspapers. However, in the main women worked exclusively from the street and if they did have regular clients who contacted them by telephone, these contacts had been made through street trade:

Lilia said she'd not really been working in the town much lately but had been just seeing her regulars. These men had a note of her telephone number. 'I don't like giving them my address like straightaway, you know, because I've got to live here, so . . . and they're all OK, you know, they always phone up first and make sure, you know, that they've got an appointment booked, get it all organized then I know who's coming, when, and they all know the price before they come here so there's no' like wrangling about how much and that.'

Estimating prostitute numbers

When we began this research there were no methods for reliably estimating the number of women working on the streets in any given area. To some this may hardly seem a significant deficiency; however, as we noted in our introduction, our research began with the concern to estimate the extent of HIV infection among streetworking prostitutes. Previous research studies, both in the UK and elsewhere, have reported information on the percentage of female prostitutes tested who were shown to have HIV infection (we summarize much of this information in Chapter 5). Testing a given number of women and finding that a certain percentage are HIV positive is only really meaningful if one also has some estimate of the size of the population being referred to: 10 per cent of 100 people being HIV positive is one thing whereas 10 per cent of 1000 being HIV positive is quite another. In the first two years of our research we developed a method for estimating the total number of women working on the streets and the proportion who were injecting drugs. The latter information was important given that previous research had shown that prostitutes involved in injecting drug use were at much higher risk of HIV than non-drug-injecting prostitutes. We look at the impact of drug injecting on the street prostitution scene in Glasgow in Chapter 3.

It is worth briefly describing the approach we developed for estimating the

Table 1   Number of prostitutes contacted and number of times contacted

	Year 1	Year 2
Number of women contacted	194	167
Total number of contacts	1078	812

number of women working in the area. During each evening's work we would walk around the entire set of streets comprising the red-light area, approach as many women whom we observed working as possible and offer them the condoms, sterile needles etc. In return we asked all women to provide us with a unique identifier (a mix of their initials and the day and the month that they were born on). Through this means we were able to build up a profile not only of the total number of women working each night over the months of our fieldwork, but also of the specific women contacted. In Table 1 we summarize the data on the number of women contacted in the first two years of our research.

The approach we were using in analysing the unique identifier information was basically a social variant of the approach used by field ecologists to estimate bird and fish populations. Field ecologists typically capture a sample of birds, tag them, release them into the wild, capture a second sample and identify the proportion of birds in the second sample that are carrying tags from the first occasion of having been caught. The proportion of wild birds tagged in the second sample allows one to estimate what the overall population of birds within the given area must be – the bigger the overlap the smaller the population must be. In our own work the identifiers provided by the women played the same function as the tags on birds. Each evening's fieldwork could be likened to a fishing exercise with each list of identifiers provided by the women akin to the sample of fish caught. By analysing the frequency with which the same identifiers were appearing over all of the nights of our fieldwork it was possible to statistically model the size of the streetworking population over a 12-month period. (For a fuller description of this work see McKeganey *et al.* 1992; Leyland *et al.* 1993). In the second year of fieldwork we calculated that there must be in the region of 425 women working in the area.

The unique identifier information was also of value in allowing us to look at the pattern of working within the area. In Figure 1 we summarize the data on the frequency with which women were contacted in the first year of our fieldwork. What the figure shows very clearly is that the street prostitute population in Glasgow consisted of a small group of women who were working very frequently, in some cases virtually every night, and a much larger group of women who were working quite infrequently. This latter information was potentially of value in combining with information on HIV infection among the women. Our own data in this respect was anonymous and so it was not possible to look at the frequency of working of different women in terms of their HIV status; had the information from the HIV testing component of our

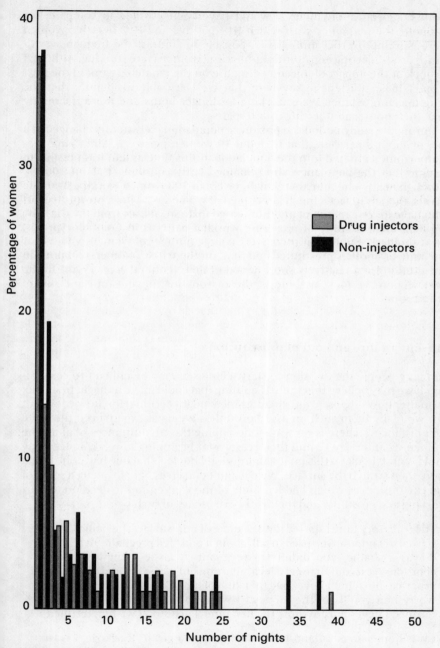

Figure 1   Working patterns of female prostitutes (observations made over 53 nights)

work not been anonymous it would have been possible to compare, for example, the frequency with which HIV positive and HIV negative women were working. In this study it was possible to contrast the frequency with which drug-injecting and non-drug-injecting women were working. Although we look at the impact of injecting drug use on the women's work in the next chapter it is sufficient to say here that we were able to identify that the drug-injecting women were working for longer hours and more frequently than their non-drug-injecting counterparts.

During the study period the prostitute population consistently changed at a rate of about 8 per cent, that is, about 19 women per week. Since almost as many women entered into the population at this time as left, it is possible to assume that the population size remained fairly constant at about 200. So although at any one time there might be about 200 women working from the streets, there is in fact a much larger pool of women who have prostituted but who have for one reason or another ceased to do so, at least from the Glasgow red-light area. A study of prostitute working patterns in Colorado Springs, USA, similiarly found that there were a large number of women who had at one time or another prostituted and that, on the whole, women remained in prostitution for a relatively short period of time (Potterat *et al.* 1990). In the next section we look at some of the reasons for moving into and out of prostitution.

Movement into and out of prostitution

To many people the decision to start selling sex may be difficult to comprehend; we may believe that there is nothing that could make us begin to sell sex no matter how desperate our circumstances might become. But how confident can we really be in such an assertion unless we have experienced the same circumstances? There is no way of describing the circumstances of all of the women we interviewed and their reasons for beginning to work; indeed one could write a book on this topic alone and still not feel that one had done much more than scratch the surface. We will limit ourselves here to giving a sense of the circumstances which had led some of the women to the decision to start working as a prostitute and their early experience of such work:

> The true story how I started it was a mate of mine in fact she helped me get started in London. She used to talk about it and I fell pregnant. At that time it was a shame, you didn't fall pregnant. A lassie I knew was daen' abortions, you couldnae get a legal abortion but it cost 30 quid, that was 21 years ago now, but I never had that kind of money. She used to say: 'Don't worry hen you'll get the money.' I went up with her one night, I was terrified I never did anything the first time. I just stood wi' her, terrified.

> I was homeless at 16 and I was staying with a girl in Ruchazie, I wasn't getting any money from the social security because I was under 18, all I had was my lodging allowance and she was threatening to throw me out if I didnae get any money. She'd been on the street before and basically it

was a case of either I did it or I was out on the street. I did it for about three weeks and that was it I couldnae do it any more.

In the following field extract, the woman described her entrance into prostitution as through a pimp in London. It should be noted, however, that in Glasgow none of the women were in the control of pimps:

I was 14 and I'd run away from home. I ended up down in London where I met a pimp. He was a really nice guy, started me working and that was it I was on the street. He'd got me a place to stay, buying me things and everything and I ended up sleeping with him as well. One night we got really drunk and stoned and he brought someone in. At the time I'd thought sex was . . . the way I'd seen it . . . then after it happened I thought it was bad, I didn't like it but at least I was getting paid for it. I'd been abused by my grandad when I was 11 and it didn't seem a million miles from that anyway.

Although the women's first attempts at prostituting were often far from positive they had, however painfully and inexpertly, been paid for sex and as a result had crossed a divide – thereafter their own body would always be seen as having the potential for generating an income:

Well I was stayin' with Gerry, I wasn't gettin' any money, we were living off about £60 a fortnight from the social and I mean there was just no money. I'd matured a lot since the first time I'd done it [worked for three weeks when she was 16] and this time it was my decision, nobody was forcin' me which made it a lot easier. At first when I mentioned it to Gerry he was dead against it, we'd had a big fight about money, but that was it I went out and I started back.

It is a commonplace belief that women beginning to prostitute will be shown the ropes by an experienced, older hand:

Ma first punter was horrible. Annie [friend] was with me, she'd stop the punters and say, 'Listen this is ma pal, she's just started doin' this.' She'd sit in the back seat of the car while I done it which was good of her but at the same time she was gettin' half of it at the end of the night.

It was not the case that all of the women were introduced to the work of being a prostitute in this way. In the course of our fieldwork we met numerous women who were beginning to work entirely on their own:

We approached a woman standing in jeans, sweatshirt and holding a red book. At first I was not sure she was working – when we spoke to her it became clear she was. She said it was her first time and that she had not even had her first punter. We told her about the prostitute drop-in operating in the area, where it was etc. and Marina went on to explain about the various different condoms for oral, vaginal, anal sex. The woman commented how embarrassed she was: 'If it wasn't so dark you'd see how red I am.' She then said that she hadn't a clue as to what to do. This is the second time we have seen a woman on her first night and both times we have had an incredible sense of their vulnerability . . . Towards the end of the evening we saw her again, she explained that a guy in a van had called over to her but that she had been too scared to respond. I suggested that maybe she should quit for the night to which she responded, 'No if I don't do it now I never will.'

We saw Tina again late last night standing next to a woman dressed in a black mini-skirted suit who was sitting rather primly on a low wall. She was new to us and she said it was her first night. Marina said she looked a bit green and the woman said she was really nervous. As Marina was running through the different condoms Tina who is a bit of a drinker rather unhelpfully interjected 'Forget-Me-Not' [brand name of one of the condoms], 'that is what you tell your last punter' [laughs]. I frequently have the impression that Tina's brain is totally addled with alcohol. She repeated her dictum a few minutes later. As we turned to leave, the woman leant towards us, tears filled her eyes and she said, 'I've never done anything like this before.' Marina said that she should ask Tina – 'She'll keep you right' – to which Tina responded, 'Keep you right? I cannae even keep mysel' right hen.'

We approached a girl working in one of the side streets. She said it was her first night out and that she had not yet done any business. She said she had friends who did it and they told her it wasn't hard to earn some money this way. They'd also told her something of the way things work. She knew for example some of the phrases to describe the scene. In other respects she seemed naïve and asked us about where it was OK for her to work. I said I thought it was OK to work if that corner or patch was vacant. One of the older women basically confirmed this though she did say that a lot depended upon the woman herself – she said she was surprised that the young girl was on her own since generally they came down with a pal who helped them do it.

According to some of the older, more experienced women, the red-light area itself had changed immeasurably over the last few years; with the influx of large numbers of individuals working to finance a drug habit much of the shared experience of work and the sense of cohesion between prostitutes had been eroded. Within such a context it is perhaps hardly surprising that many women were beginning to work without the support of an older, more experienced hand.

Stated in its broadest terms, women prostitute to make money. That is why women go to the streets to sell sex. Prostitution offers a means of earning a good income where otherwise employment opportunities might be considered limited and low wages the norm. However, as might be predicted, there are many different reasons for a woman needing that money and these have an influence over such factors as the regularity with which a woman will work and the amount of time she might spend doing so. Some women will only prostitute to supplement their income and only at those times when they need extra finance, perhaps when they have bills to pay or seasonal costs to meet:

We met a woman who says she only rarely came out to work, she mentioned Christmas as being the factor motivating her to come out: 'I wish as I could get it so as I only had to come out once every five years rather than once a year.'

Debt was a reason why some women began prostituting, as in the case of a young woman whose use of credit cards had resulted in her incurring huge debts and seeing no other way of clearing them than through prostitution:

> She said she'd begun prostituting herself because she was heavily in debt and had to pay back all the money she owed to various credit card companies. Initially her parents had baled her out 'but you take it for granted don't you?' She'd come down with a friend who already worked the town but she felt very nervous about it and also ashamed. She was really afraid of anyone finding out and her self-esteem was at rock bottom. She couldn't put a figure on the times she'd knocked back punters because she couldn't face doing anything with them: 'I used to talk about people working down here, I didn't know how they could do it, but now look at me.'

Pregnancy was another factor which could influence the frequency and duration of prostitute working hours. However women's response to pregnancy was by no means predictable. Some women immediately ceased to sell sexual services at least until the child was born and later. Some other women while perhaps not prostituting quite so frequently would continue to work until late on in pregnancy. One woman worked almost until the birth of her child:

> Catherine is very heavily pregnant and still working. She wears all black clothing to try to disguise how pregnant she is. When I asked her if it made much difference to her business she said that most clients didn't even notice, especially if she did them outside in the darker lanes.

Many women started and stopped working on the basis of the changing circumstances of their drug use. Where their habit increased women would be seen working more often; equally, on occasion, drug-using women would be arrested or spend a period undergoing drug detoxification with the result that their work on the streets would be temporarily interrupted.

Prostitution, particularly on the street, has a fluid dynamic created by the individual women who participate in it regularly or irregularly, for shorter or longer time periods. It is spatially limited by the boundaries the police have set, and the police also have some influence over what is and what is not acceptable within the area. Other than this women appear to come and go according to their perceived needs and preferences.

Relationships between the women and notions of professionalism

Relations between the women were at one and the same time communal and competitive, friendly and fractious. The communal aspect of relations between the women was most impressively illustrated on those occasions when individual women could be heard having trouble with a client. At such times other women would converge on the scene without regard for their own safety to offer whatever help they could. Relations between the women were far from universally positive however. There were fractious disputes between drug-injecting and non-drug-injecting women:

> I cannae stand being with all the junkies, always full of it and some of them can hardly speak. I'd like to just punch them in the face so I would. They're the ones doing it without a condom, them and the old ones that cannae get a man any other way.

When Neil and I met Danni at the beginning of the evening she talked about having an abscess in her groin which was painful. By the end of the evening she was in agony. Finally the police, on finding her lying on the floor, radioed for an ambulance. Whilst lying on the floor one of the non-injecting women [Fiona] came over. She is a particularly abrasive person and very anti-drugs. Seeing Danni on the floor she said aloud that it was her own fault. To this Danni replied, 'You don't know what it is like when you have a habit to feed.' Fiona then made another comment about drug users working in the area to a drug-injecting woman who was standing nearby. She feistily replied that she was not a junkie, that she did not have a habit and that she had a wean [child] to look after. Another woman commented that Fiona was not really in a position to talk since she was working as a prostitute anyway. At this Fiona seemed to back down saying she too had a wean to look after.

The fault lines among the women, however, had to do with a good deal more than the matter of drug injecting. Women who were new to the area, particularly if they were seen to be successful at attracting clients, could also attract criticism from injecting and non-injecting women alike:

> As we were standing with a group, one of the women pointed at a prostitute who was walking on the opposite side of the road to us. The group watched her every move as she adopted a sexy hip-swaying walk and then stopped to look at herself in the shop window. 'Who the fuck does she think she is, a model on the catwalk or what?' one of the women commented. The women bristled as she took a brush out and tidied her hair. 'She doesn't even have a bag to keep her condoms in, she must be keeping them in her bra to dodge the polis,' one of the other women said. Marina went over to give the woman condoms and stood chatting to her for a while. It turned out that she had recently moved to Glasgow from London to get away from her pimp.

Negative comments would also be made about women who were felt to be working in the area without sufficient regard for their appearance:

> Another woman walked by and both of the two women I was talking to expressed their disapproval of her — saying she was 'boggin' [dirty] and that she'd been wearing the same skirt for the past few nights and it was all

stained from her sexual contacts with clients. The other agreed saying she knew that she slept in her make-up and just touched it up the next day.

Some of the women clearly had a notion of professionalism which included judgements to do with standards of behaviour and dress which they felt some women were failing to match up to.

The potentially fractious relationships between women could also be seen in the way in which they would conceal from each other how much money they were making:

> I asked Elizabeth how much business she had done that night. She said £70 and added, 'I'll tell you that, I'd have said one or two if anyone else had asked or I'd have said I hadn't done any.' She said she always underestimated if other women asked how much money she had made.

It is easy to see why the issue of money should have been so sensitive. All of the women were aware that they were constantly a target for street violence and for that reason alone would not want to advertise the fact of carrying large sums of money. In addition a woman who was earning large amounts of money could be seen as reducing the earning potential of all of the other women in the area. For this reason the women would not draw attention to how much money they had earned.

In their relationships with each other one had a sense of both the individuality in the women's work and their strong links with the other women with whom they shared the experience of working as a prostitute. The competitiveness between women undoubtedly strained relationships but it did not preclude them. What tended to happen was that women would strike up a relationship with one or two others working nearby while keeping other women at a distance. This made the issue of 'working spots' particularly important. Although it was never entirely clear whether a system of spots operated in the area it was the case that the same women would be seen working the same area on successive nights. How vigorously these spots would be defended seemed to depend in large part on the individuals concerned. Some women undoubtedly did defend their area while others seemed rather more tolerant.

The experience of selling sex

To get some idea of the kind of sex being sold we can look at the small survey of 66 working women we carried out as part of our work. The women's ages ranged from 16 to 51, the average being 24. The average length of time the women had worked as a prostitute was two years, ranging from one night to 30 years. The women worked an average of five nights a week and had approximately seven clients per night.

In Table 2 we summarize the data on sexual services sold by the women on the last night they worked. These figures confirm the impression conveyed in our informal street interviews with the women; oral sex was the service which the women were asked to provide most often. This preference for oral sex was

Table 2   Sexual services provided on most recent night worked
(*n* = 66)

Sexual service	Total	Average per woman
Vaginal sex	147	2.2
Oral sex	200	3.0
Anal sex	0	0
Masturbation	58	0.9

shared by at least some of the women who commented to us that it posed less of a risk in terms of HIV:

> One woman said that she had stopped doing sex with clients and now only did gams [oral sex]. She said that four and a half months ago a condom had burst during full sex. As a result she felt that sex was too dangerous. She had had an HIV test in response to this and the test had been negative.

None of the women we interviewed said that they provided anal sex although all of them reported regularly being asked for this by clients. Such comments as the following were typical:

> I never let a punter do anal, never. I tried it once with ma boyfriend and it was so painful I never done it again.

> Anal sex is a definite no. I wouldnae even do that with ma boyfriend, tell the truth I did once with one of the guys I was engaged to and I was roarin' and greetin' [crying] and he was goin' 'sorry, sorry, I'm so sorry.'

It is difficult to know what to make of such statements. The fact that anal sex was being asked for so widely suggests that some men were probably successful in their attempts at buying this service. This interpretation certainly accords with the information provided by the clients which we present in the following chapter. It is also in accord with some of the things women were overheard saying:

> Neil inadvertently heard a conversation between two women. One was complaining about how long a punter had taken to orgasm. The other replied that she had had a similar case and she had told him to 'slip it up the back passage'. This, she pointed out, had speedily concluded the business.

According to the women, a request for anal sex was one of the most common reasons for turning down a client. There were numerous occasions in our fieldwork where we observed this happening:

> As Marina and I were walking up the street I watched a guy 20 or 30 yards in front approach Anita. The two spoke briefly then he wandered off. As he did so Anita shouted over to us – and anyone else in the vicinity – 'Anal, he wanted anal.' You could almost feel the guy's embarrassment as he walked

down the hill. Anita for her part was clearly not prepared to even consider providing anal sex.

It was clear in our interviews that many women had made a decision in their own mind as to what they would and would not be prepared to do in the course of their work:

> Irene said she found the idea of kissing clients totally repulsive: 'It's bad enough when they're stabbing into your ear trying to get you going, kissing, no way.'

Other women had ruled out other sexual acts:

> I don't do sex, I don't do anal, anything with sex at all. I don't like punters touching me, I'll touch them but no ways like them touchin' me, it makes me cringe. I'd rather do what they want and that's it.

> Most nights you don't get asked for sex up your bum but some nights you do. I don't suck people's balls, I don't do that. I won't let them put their fingers inside me.

> This guy said 'gonnae pee on me?' And I was like that [shocked]. I said, 'Could you say that again?' And he said, 'I need you to pee in ma face.' I said, 'And in the meantime, while I'm peein' in your face, what are you gonnae be doin'?' and he said, 'I'm going to open ma mouth and catch it.' I said, 'You're no' gonnae catch ma pee you bastard, get to fuck out of here.' He was gonnae catch ma pee in his mouth – is that sick or is that sick?

Not all of the clients' requests involved sex. Sometimes the clients would simply wish to talk to the prostitute or spend some time with her:

> We bumped into Clare who regaled us with a story of having just been approached by a transvestite who asked if she would walk down Sauchiehall Street with him. She had agreed [easy money she said]. As the two had been walking down the street they had been stopped by two vice cops. Clare said the guy 'had just about shit himself' and that she had asked them if it was not a crime to go walking in the street. She had obviously found the whole thing pretty funny.

> A woman pulled me over to one side saying that a punter had just bought her pants for £10. She said she'd never done that before and felt a bit weird standing there with no pants on under her skirt. She then said that last night a guy had asked her to 'do toilet in a bag' for him. She said she couldn't do it: 'Some things are private, I wasnae gonnae do that in front of him or anybody.'

These non-sexual acts were often favoured by women as a relatively easy source of money.

Negotiating sex

At the heart of the prostitute/client encounter are three considerations: the woman's decision as to what she would be prepared to do; the nature of the client's request; and the amount of money on offer. Each of these elements had an impact on each other:

> Two guys approached as we were standing chatting to Tina – one of them said that they wanted Tina to appear at a job interview for one of their friends as a prank. Tina shook her head – not for 40 quid I won't.

> I was working last night and this guy was tryin' to get a gam [oral sex] for a fiver. I mean there's no way I'm gonnae accept that – a gam for a fiver, no matter how hard up I am I've got ma pride, I'm not doin' it for that.

It was the compromise between these three things which enabled sex to be sold. Moreover the rules of the game were not fixed; what a client or a woman might accept depended in part on the individual circumstances at any one time. This fact alone made the negotiation between prostitute and client all the more important.

Once a car stopped women would initiate a fairly standard introduction which typically consisted of asking the motorist if he was 'looking for business'. The language is important here since it unambiguously identifies the woman as selling sex. There were occasions during our fieldwork when clients were observed approaching women in a way that could best be described as ambiguous; the women's response to such approaches would invariably be to cut through any ambiguity and state very clearly the nature of the work they were involved in:

> As we talked with Marcie, a man crossed over the road and made to talk to her. Holding an unlit cigarette, he directly asked Marcie, 'You got a light, doll?' Without batting an eyelid she responded, 'Aye and I don't do it outside by the way'. Whereas he had tried to initiate contact in terms more usual in non-commerical contacts, a pick-up line in a disco, perhaps, she had immediately cut through all of that and established it firmly as a commerical contact.

Once it had been established that the client was looking to buy sex, negotiation as to the kind of sex on offer and price could begin in earnest. Some of the women would establish the specifics of this negotiation at the kerbside before entering the client's car, others would do it on the way to the venue where sex would be traded:

> You go over and if it's a regular you jump in the car, if its no' a regular you say where are you wanting it – in the car or in the flat. They'll ask you how much and I'll say what you wantin', if he's wantin' oral it's so much, if he's wantin' something kinky I'll work out a price, if he's wantin' a certain length of time I'll work that out and tell him the price, if he agrees, that's you.

Throughout the process of negotiation the women adopt an assertive, businesslike stance. Through taking charge right from the beginning, the women hope to secure client compliance; as vendors of a desired service, the women consider themselves to be in a position to dictate the terms and conditions of that sale. A large part of the rationale for this resides in an acute awareness of the potential dangers of providing sex to men who for the most part are total strangers. By setting the terms of the transaction the women aim to take and retain control of the situation thereby, hopefully, lessening the chances that the clients will attempt to usurp them. The issue of control was very prominent in the minds of the women and was directly linked both to ensuring payment and to notions of personal safety:

> Because if you're puttin' it across to the punters that you're a wee timorous wee thing, they're gonnae treat you like a mug, they will and I think that's trouble. I don't get much hassle 'cos they can see that I'm straight. I'm compos mentis all the time and that and very matter of fact about it, you know, I don't mess about.

The journey to the venue where sex would be provided was itself a crucial part of the process of selling sex on the streets. The women would almost always decide themselves the place where sex would be provided, often giving the driver precise directions as to the route to take. Such directions were one way in which the women could assess the possible risk a client might represent:

> Tania was chatting about an incident on a previous night when a woman had been attacked by two guys one of whom had emerged from the boot of the car once they had arrived at the spot where sex was to be provided. Tania said that she always checked the back seat of cars in case someone was hiding there. She also described how when she gets in the car she gives clear instructions of where to go – turn left here, right here, and that on one occasion when a punter had deviated from these instructions she had put her foot through the guy's windscreen when he had turned on to the motorway.

Although such a reaction might seem extreme it does give a clear indication of the women's constant awareness of the risks they faced in their work (a risk which, as we show in Chapter 6, was very real).

Having arrived at the venue where sex would be traded there were a number of options facing the woman. Sex could proceed in precisely the way that had been agreed. Alternatively a client might take longer than expected to reach a climax, or he might request additional sexual services not initially agreed upon. The resolution of these uncertainties could produce additional income for the women depending upon how skilled they were in their work and the level of naïvety on the client's part:

> Natalie was describing how she charged. 'If he touches you then you say that's a tenner more, three touches that's £70, that's how you make your extra money.' She did add though that some of the punters were aware of such strategies and would only carry a certain amount of money on them.

> I'll say you want an extra two minutes that's £10. I work by the time – I'll say right you've been here for five minutes that's more money.

> If they start touching ma tits I say, 'You cannae do that.' They cannae get touching you without openin' your buttons. Once they start that I say it's extra for playin' around. A lot of them say, 'But I always get a play around

with a gam.' I say, 'You give me the extra or I'll stop.' I've seen me sitting up till they've handed over.

There was a fine line to be drawn between extracting maximum money from a client and causing them to feel so exploited that they became aggressive or refused to return to the woman on any subsequent occasion. Despite the obvious business sense of keeping on the right side of this line, it was one which at least a minority of women were prepared to breach on occasion:

She described having recently gone back to the flat with a drunk man. Once on the bed she had chatted and chatted until as she put it she had 'bored him to sleep'. Once asleep she had gone through his wallet and stolen £80.

With the completion of the transaction (assuming it had proceeded relatively smoothly) the client would then return the woman to the site she was working from. In some cases women described how at the end of their evening's work their last client might drive them home. Such a strategy, though saving on taxi fares, would only be initiated where the client was a regular or where the woman otherwise felt he posed no risk.

This description of the prostitute/client relationship in terms of the negotiation over sex and money gives no sense of the women's skill in attracting clients — a skill which in itself was at the heart of the women's work and in which some women excelled:

A couple of nights back both Marina and I were enormously impressed by the style of working of one of the women. We had been walking 50 or so yards behind her up a hill when a young guy was walking down the hill. As he passed the woman she immediately turned on her heels and began walking alongside him looking up at him in a way that was both playfully coy and sexually alluring. We watched this performance in silent admiration as the two passed us and then turned into a nearby alley. When we met the woman later that night I congratulated her on the power of her performance — she then laughed and said that 'if you look right into their eyes they can never say no'. As if to demonstrate this the latter was said while looking into my eyes and smiling. I could see what she meant.

Whatever one might think of the business of selling sex it was difficult not to be impressed by the skill with which some women carried out their work. Not all the women, of course, were equally interested in such a display:

We saw Anna who was standing dressed in sneakers and a shortish skirt. I asked her about clothing, particularly about wearing stilettos [which she never does]. She said she wasn't interested in wearing those kinds of clothes because she wasn't bothered about punters: 'Take it or leave it, I'm no' dressing up for they cunts.' She then said that some clients asked her why she worked in the town if she was reluctant to (a) dress for them and (b) provide many services. She said all she wanted was the money and as soon as she got that she was off.

There was no one view of clients which the women shared. Instead there was a range of views which seemed to reflect different women's experience of their work. Some of the women saw their clients in a fairly favourable light, others were much more negative in describing them. Some women described their clients solely in terms of the money they provided, others pointed out that clients were about more than that:

> A good punter is someone who is regular, pays good money and if he's a nice guy that's a good punter. Somebody that's nice you can talk to, knows how to treat you – you get some that – I want this I want that, somebody that's just nice, easy going makes me feel relaxed with, not all the money – I mean I've got good punters that don't necessarily give me lots of money and I've got bad punters that give me the money.

> You get some clients that are arrogant, cheeky, who think they can get everything for a fiver, don't care how they treat you, don't care if they thrust it in or how rough they are.

> I hate them [punters] – people will say to me I treat them like shit . . . there was a guy the other night that said, 'Can you no' treat me like a human being?' I don't know what it is but I just cannae treat them like a human being, it's just, they're perverts as far as I'm concerned. . . . You keep seein' them, it's sickening. I keep sayin' what the fuck's he coming up here fae, ye know what I mean. I'm 22 and he's about fuckin' 50 . . . They come up, talk about their wife, about their daughter . . . I'm thinkin' he's comin' up to see me and he's got a daughter the same age, does he think the same way about his daughter, you know what I mean.

Many of the most negative views of clients were held by women who were working to finance a drug habit; having said this, however, not all of the drug-injecting women saw their clients in such negative terms.

In this chapter we have covered many aspects of the business of selling sex from the negotiation with clients to the number of women working. It is clear from what we have said so far that drug injecting has had an enormous impact on the street prostitution scene in Glasgow. We look at this in greater detail in the following chapter.

3

The impact of drug use on the women's work

Introduction

In this chapter we look at the influence injecting drug use has had on the street prostitution scene in Glasgow. We look at the extent of drug injecting among the women and describe our methods for establishing whether or not women were injecting. We also describe the impact which injecting drug use had on the women's work, including how they dealt with clients' attempts to find out if they were drug injectors. In large part the clients were concerned with the question of whether the women were injecting because of their fears that the women might be HIV positive. Towards the end of the chapter we look at our data, as well as data from other studies, on the extent of needle sharing among the women.

The extent of drug injecting among street prostitutes in Glasgow

It is clear from the previous chapter that illicit drug use has an enormous impact on the street prostitution scene in Glasgow. The overlap between drug use and prostitution is not, of course, unique to Glasgow but is something which has been noted in countries throughout the world. Our interest in trying to establish the extent of drug injecting among Glasgow's street prostitutes arose from the finding of higher levels of HIV infection among drug-injecting prostitutes compared to non-drug-injecting prostitutes which has been reported in numerous studies (European Working Group on HIV Infection in Female Prostitutes 1993). Previous studies in some UK cities have identified varying levels of drug injecting among female prostitutes in different cities. Research in Edinburgh conducted in the late 1980s, for example, reported approximately 20 per cent of working women injecting drugs (Morgan Thomas *et al.* 1989). In London a figure of 14 per cent was reported by researchers in 1988 (Day *et al.* 1988) and just over 10 per cent by the same research team in 1993 (Ward *et al.* 1993). Substantially higher levels of drug injecting among female prostitutes in Manchester were reported by Faugier and her colleagues (Faugier *et al.* 1992).

The difficulty with these studies, however, is that estimates of the proportion of prostitute women injecting drugs tend to combine both streetworking and non-streetworking women. It is generally reported that women who work from the streets are more likely to inject drugs than those in off-street locations. This suggests the importance of producing separate estimates for the different settings of prostitution work. Since our own research was concentrating on streetworking women we had the opportunity of providing an estimate for that section of the prostitute population.

By offering the women sterile injecting equipment we were able to distinguish between drug-injecting and non-drug-injecting women in a way which did not rely solely on women self-reporting whether they were injecting. The possession of injecting equipment for non-medical purposes is not a criminal offence in Glasgow. However it is a reasonable assumption that women who were not injecting would not have been requesting injecting equipment from us:

> We don't usually have a great deal of contact with Elaine. She doesn't inject drugs but mentioned that her daughter does. She said she would like to get some needles from us for her daughter since she heard her saying how blunt her set was getting. 'But I cannae take any off youse, I cannae risk being found carrying them on me.'

We are confident that our estimate of the extent of injecting among streetworking women in Glasgow was not inflated by women who were not injecting but were taking injecting equipment from us. Much more likely is the possibility that some women wanted to conceal the fact of their drug injecting, as much from us as from others, such as the police:

> Our second evening back on the streets after a short break. Loads of cars driving around but only a few women. I was amazed to see a woman who I had first met in the Gorbals four years ago. At that time she had been really attractive, lively and the centre of attention. Now she was thin, incredibly drawn looking. The transformation was really shocking. I asked her how she was keeping; 'shite', she answered. I asked her if she was still hitting up [injecting] and she nodded. She then said that she had had a little boy since I'd last seen her and that he had only lived 26 hours. When we offered her condoms and tools she declined the latter saying that she had told the police she was not injecting and didn't want to be caught out lying.

By recording the unique identifier information on each of the women we contacted, and adding a notation for those who accepted injecting equipment, it was possible to build up a picture of the proportion of our contacts each night who were injecting and from that information to estimate the overall extent of injecting among women working on the streets in Glasgow. The unique

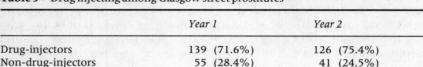

Table 3   Drug injecting among Glasgow street prostitutes

	Year 1	Year 2
Drug-injectors	139 (71.6%)	126 (75.4%)
Non-drug-injectors	55 (28.4%)	41 (24.5%)
Total number of women	194	167

identifier data also enabled us to compare the frequency with which drug-injecting prostitutes were working compared to the non-drug-injecting women.

In Table 3 we summarize our data on the drug-injecting status of the women we contacted in the first two years of our research. In the first year of the study 72 per cent of the women were injecting; in the second year, although fewer women were contacted overall, the proportion who were injecting rose to 75 per cent. These figures are considerably higher than those reported for other UK cities (with the exception of Manchester). The reasons for this are likely to be in part to do with the extent of drug injecting in Glasgow. The number of injecting drug users in the city has been estimated as approximately 8500 (Frischer 1992). This represents just less than 1 per cent of the overall Glasgow population, indicating a substantial drug problem in Glasgow. In UK terms, Glasgow probably has the largest injecting population outside of London. It does not necessarily follow, of course, that a woman injecting drugs will inevitably prostitute to finance her drug use. However, the fact that Glasgow has a large injecting population (of whom one in three are estimated to be women) probably goes some way towards explaining the large number of drug-injecting prostitutes working in the city.

As well as being in the majority, drug-injecting women were also working more frequently and for longer periods of time than their non-drug-injecting counterparts. So, for example, in 1992 a total of 139 drug-injectors were contacted 755 times. A total of 55 non-injecting prostitute women (28.4 per cent of the population) were seen in total 323 times.

The pressures of earning sufficient money to finance a drug addiction were a large part of the explanation for the greater frequency with which drug-injecting women were observed to be working:

> She said that business had been awful that night: 'Worst it's ever been I think.' She said she had to get £55 by 4.30 a.m. [it was then nearly 3 a.m.], she had to deliver it to a house [repaying a debt]. She also needed at least £40 for herself: 'At least that'll square me up, it'll take away the pain.'

> Isobel told us she was 'feart [frightened] to work,' [she had earlier that week been savagely attacked by a client] but added, 'But when you've a habit to feed you've got to.'

Although non-drug-injecting prostitutes might have other expenses to meet which might at times be pressing, in general they were never as financially pressurized.

A factor contributing to the greater frequency with which drug-injecting women were observed to be working relates to the fact that many of these women had sexual partners who were also injecting. Often women reported that they prostituted to finance not just their drug habit but that of their partner as well:

'He doesnae need it every day but I do, so I have to come out. Ma habit's heavier than his.' She's also paying for his drug habit.

In part this was because the women recognized their greater earning power through selling sex than through living off the proceeds of petty theft. In part it was to avoid the increased possibility of their partners going to jail should they rely on shoplifting or burglary to generate income. This was very clearly how one woman had rationalized it:

Belinda is always pretty busy, I guess because she really dresses the part. The other night she referred to her money saying she'd made £100, gone home to score and then came out and earned a further £150. I asked her if she supported his habit. She looked skyward – 'Aye.' She discourages him from shoplifting: 'I says to him, it's not worth it, it's better if I do it for the both of us, he only gets the jail for it.'

Hardly any of the non-drug-injecting women we contacted said that they were working to finance a partner's drug habit although this has been reported for other UK cities. During the course of this study, only two women reported prostituting to fund a boyfriend's or husband's drug addiction without being similarly involved in drugs:

Marsha told us she had just started working the town and that she was doing it to support her man (he's an injector). 'It was either that or the jail for him and I wanted tae keep him out. I mean I knew he was a junkie when I started wi' him, so I knew what I was taking on. I love him to bits, it had to be done.'

Perhaps it is noteworthy that when we interviewed the same woman a couple of years later she reframed her motivation for becoming involved in prostitution. At this point she described it as an entirely personal decision to have an independent source of income:

'Well I was staying with Phil and I still wasn't getting any money, we were living off about £60 a fortnight giro [social security] from him, he was supplying everything, there was no money; I mean there was just no money. I was a lot more mature then, I'd been in a hospital a lot and I managed to sort myself out and I'd matured a lot and this time it was my decision so I think that made it a lot easier, 'cos nobody was forcing me to do it, I was the one that said to Phil, 'I'm gonnae go out and work,' and he's goin', 'No you're not,' and I said, 'I'm going out to work whether you like it or you don't like it. I mean I need these shoes, I need these clothes, I need these underwear, I need. . . .' I mean you can't buy it off £56 a fortnight and I spoke to Angela [his sister] quite a bit about it and she was against it, me going out you know, the two of them were totally against it 'cos they had both known about my previous experience and thought no.' [She had at an earlier age been pushed into prostitution by a female friend.] 'Well I just got ready one night . . .'

This contrasted sharply with the reasoning provided at the time when she had just entered into prostitution. Whatever the rationale for her prostituting, it was she who took responsibility for providing money for his drug addiction. This was negatively perceived by other prostitutes, including some women who were drug-injectors themselves. In the following field diary extract two women were discussing Marsha who at the time was over eight months pregnant and still prostituting:

Ella and Amanda were talking about a woman who's pregnant and still working as a prostitute, even though she's due in three weeks' time. The conversation then turned to her boyfriend. He's an injecting drug user. Amanda said, 'What gets me is that he's at home in the warm with his feet up while she's out here freezing in the cold.' They think she's working to feed his drug habit, as in fact do many of the women. Ella said disdainfully, 'Aye, leeches the lot of them.' She couldn't understand how Marsha stayed with her boyfriend. 'How does she do it? She should sling him.'

The obvious disdain with which these and other women regarded Marsha's reasons for prostituting (although not her personally) may perhaps have been a factor contributing to Marsha's changed rationale for prostituting.

Street prostitution, at least in Glasgow, seems to be characterized by constant fluctuations not only in the numbers of women working on any one night but in individual women's working patterns. Some women worked very frequently in one year of the study but were hardly seen the next, some were only ever seen intermittently. Through being in the area over time we were able to build up a picture of the various factors influencing this movement, particularly among the drug-injectors. We consider some of these in the following section.

Drug-injecting prostitutes often report on the escalation of their drug consumption (and so also the cost) when they are prostituting. It has been reported elsewhere that there is an equivalence between the size and cost of a drug-injecting habit and the amount of money available to service that habit (Fields and Walters 1985). Drug addiction does not therefore *necessarily* entail ever greater expenditure. However, prostitution can generate relatively large sums of money over a short period of time, certainly more than most might otherwise expect. Street women regularly reported earning in excess of a hundred pounds for a few hours' work. Apart from putting aside money for necessities, travel to and from work and cigarettes, many drug-injectors said that they used as much money as they had available for drugs:

When Elaine mentioned how much money she'd made on the last night she'd worked, I asked her if that meant she'd had money left over for the next day [I suppose I was thinking she wouldn't have to work every night if she did well on certain nights]. At this she just shrugged and said,

'The more money you make the more you spend, you just get a bigger habit, that's all.'

In a relatively short period of time a woman can develop a large drug habit. In turn this puts increased pressure on her to work more frequently and for longer hours. Many women recognized a certain inevitability to this cycle:

During the time she was off drugs she didn't prostitute, then her habit began again and she began to work the streets. 'You do it 'cos you need the money but then you get a big habit so you have to keep coming out.'

The increased financial pressure which drug-injecting prostitutes are often under has been linked to increased risk-taking (Vanwesenbeeck *et al.* 1994) and, specifically, to a reduced likelihood of consistent condom use with clients (Gossop *et al.* 1995). This was certainly a charge levelled by many of the non-drug-using prostitutes. However, the point has also been made that the higher frequencies of unprotected sex among injecting prostitutes may just be a feature of their tendency to work for longer hours to boost their earnings (Bloor 1995).

There were some women who were able to retain control over their habit, whether through only using certain substances, or more unusually by regulating the amount used:

Linda said that Lorna was only in need of one more client. 'That's all she needs, the one and then that'll be her, see she's already done one so she only needs the one more. £30 a day, that's all we need, £15 for Tems [Temgesics] and £15 for fags, fares and a bit of food.' She went on to explain that with Tems you didn't need to spend so much: 'Don't get me wrong, you can have loads of them, with Tems you don't get like that' [she gestured being really stoned] 'but it's still a habit and it still costs you. Thank God I've no' got a £70 or £80 habit like some of the lassies down here using smack'.

Talking with a woman whom I know to be an injector I asked her how she managed to come out here so infrequently. 'See I buy a big lot [of heroin] at one go. I don't mess around with small deals. Then I divide it into piles and use some each day.' I was amazed at her self-control and wondered if she didn't get greedy. 'Aye, well, when I first get it I get a right good dig out o' it but then I ration mysel'.'

Once a drug habit becomes large and therefore increasingly expensive to service, many women find the pressures of their drug dependence difficult to sustain. For some this may motivate them to detoxify from drugs. This is what Rosenbaum (1981) describes as 'burn-out'. Similarly, women who regularly work for longer periods greatly increase their chances of being apprehended by police and being fined by the law courts. For some women these fines go unpaid, particularly if they are trying to service a spiralling drug habit as well as attend various other needs, for example childcare. As fines mount up so prostitutes become liable to imprisonment for non-payment if they do not immediately pay off their court fines. Many women, during the course of this study, reported having 'a warrant out' on them and would try to avoid police attention. However, inevitably they would be caught and if they could not find the money they would be imprisoned. For some women a spell in prison was something of a relief as they would detoxify from drugs and generally be free of the pressures of drug addiction and prostitution. Drug detoxification or imprisonment were two common reasons for women to stop prostituting for periods of time. Even if it was only a temporary break in drug use and a woman began again to inject drugs and also to prostitute, her tolerance for drugs would be lower and subsequently the size and cost of her drug habit, at least in the short-term, would be less demanding.

It was also apparently the case that some women would 'mature out' of drug addiction. Such a process was reported by Stimson and Oppenheimer (1982) in a longitudinal study of drug injectors in London. Over time (about ten years in the London study) some injectors either gradually or suddenly become sufficiently disaffected with drug use and its associated lifestyle to stop their involvement. In the case of at least one woman ceased involvement in drug injecting led to her gradual move away from prostitution until she stopped altogether:

> Last time Sandy was out she said she was not really working much any more because she didn't really feel like it. I asked if that meant difficulty feeding her drug habit [and that of her boyfriend]. She said no, she didn't really have much of a habit any more and nor did he. She added that she'd been hitting up for nine years now and with her daughter getting to an age when she noticed those kinds of things she wanted to stop.

It is generally reported that drug-injecting women only prostitute to finance their drug habit and to a large extent this was the case among Glasgow streetworkers. Many of the women we interviewed stated the belief that if they had been able to overcome their drug dependence they would immediately cease working:

> If I stopped working you'd never see me there again, never, I wouldnae even pass by there if I was out getting my messages [shopping] or getting clothes. I wouldnae pass by.

Despite the strength of such feeling it was clear that the very interdependence between the women's work and their drug use made the task of breaking that circle all but impossible for many women; they worked to finance their drug use and they used their drugs to enable them to work:

> If I've no' had a hit I just want the work over and done with, if you've had a hit you can stand the work no bother – it doesnae bother you. But if you're straight you start to think about it, things start flooding back intae your mind.

During the times that they were not injecting drugs, some women did report not working as prostitutes. However, there were women who did not fit this pattern:

> The woman we met last night had injected drugs for two years until she was 19. Then she and her boyfriend had decided to stop, had done 'cold

turkey' and ceased injecting. She's now 24. She said that every now and again they had taken some heroin but had never injected again. Now she doesn't use it at all.

One woman considered that her drug use had effectively barred her from seeking legitimate employment:

> We met a woman who looked quite different to many of the women as she was very smartly turned out. She said she'd been an addict until five years ago. 'I jus' come out every now and again when I need the money. I cannae get a job 'cos of the state of ma hands with track marks all over them.'

Other women, who had once been injectors but had continued to prostitute, framed their reasons in terms of the greater earning power afforded them by prostitution:

> I was talking about using prostitution to fund things other than drugs; she answered, 'Aye that's true, I know 'cos I used to take drugs but you get used to the money. You need it for bills and so you come out.'

Any discussion of injecting drug use cannot avoid the possibility of drug overdose. During the course of this fieldwork a total of five women died through drug overdoses and at least two others narrowly avoided death through early discovery and medical treatment. Two prostitute women were murdered during the course of the study period; at least one of the murders was drug-related.

The impact of drugs on the women's work

The relationship between the women's work and their drug use was complex. The fact that the women were seen to be able to earn substantial sums of money meant they would be offered drugs on credit by dealers confident of their ability to pay for past drugs used. This inevitably increased the pressure on some women to continue working:

> For the past week, like last Monday, I'd been earning £150 every night. That's what I'd be earning but part of that is debt money – no' in debt ways but drug debt, payin' back for drugs I've had.

It is difficult to overstate the extent of the pressure which the drug-injecting women in particular were working under. Some measure of this can perhaps be gleaned from the example of one woman, Lesley:

> Lesley told us she had to go to court tomorrow because she had been ordered to pay two outstanding fines totalling £112. She appeared to find this a tall order since she still had to find the money to pay for her habit.'I've still got to get the money for ma kit [heroin] and I'm keepin' his [habit] going as well, so that's a hundred at least, aye well £80 for ma kit and then about £30 for jellies [temazepam] as well.' She said she had a giro coming tomorrow for £60 which meant she had only to earn about £150 or

so although she also needed £10 for fags etc. I mentioned food; 'Food,' she retorted, 'last thing on ma mind food is.'

Drug use was not only incorporated into the women's routines for preparing to work and for coming home from work. In much the same way as has been reported for other cities (Hunt 1990) drugs and drug dealing were an integral part of the red-light area itself. There were always dealers in the area ready to sell women drugs once they had earned sufficient money to pay for them. Also the partners of the women and the women themselves sold drugs:

> Another woman came over and offered the woman we were standing with the opportunity to buy drugs. She was selling Temgesic and temazepam. She ordered a tray of Temgesics [ten for £35] and warned her not to rip her off. The woman assured her she wouldn't because it was her boyfriend that was selling them.

> Rena was chatting away about making a good bit of money that night. Her boyfriend sits in a Volvo on the other side of the road and waits for her. Apparently he'd bought a gram of heroin which he had stashed and they were selling it to the women [or anyone else that was looking for it]. They'd made up four bags to sell and would supplement it with Rena's income from prostitution.

There was also a steady stream of taxis ferrying the women to other parts of the city where drugs could be purchased:

> Loretta was in a good humour saying she'd earned a good bit of money. She added excitely 'I've got ma jellies [temazepam].' Earlier we noticed a Rover pulled up with two guys in it. Carly was first off negotiating in the window and then she must have agreed the deal because she got in the car and he handed something over to her. The other guy stayed outside of the motor.

It was not difficult to see the visible signs of such widespread drug use among the women. On virtually every night of our fieldwork there were women working who could barely stand up and who would either stagger from street to street or lean precariously against one of the buildings waiting for a client to drive by:

> Every time we see Nan nowadays she looks worse. She's recognizable chiefly by the way her body stoops forward. When I asked her yesterday if she wanted needles she looked at me for a long time with a totally vacant stare. Just as I was beginning to wonder if she was all right she told me she did want some needles. It's hard to believe the transformation in her in so short a time. She can only have been working the town for about six months.

It was not only the drug-injecting women who were working in such circumstances however:

> We saw Irene and Tania tonight, both were completely off their skulls with drink. Tania was almost paralytic. How she could do business I don't know.

She could barely stand or speak. The only thing she kept slurring to me was 'all men are bastards'.

In some ways it might seem rather odd that women working in such conditions would still be able to attract clients. On the basis of our observations within the area there appeared to be no shortage of clients picking up such women. It is possible that some clients may have been attracted to these women precisely because of their apparent inability to control the transaction as a result of the effects of their drug use.

Where women were so clearly drugged it was difficult to believe that they had sufficient consciousness to know what they were doing. This is evident from the next two field extracts. In the first, the woman herself describes not knowing what she was doing and in the second another woman describes the financial costs of being so drugged:

> She never injected eggs [temazepam] but swallowed them and said that yesterday she was 'walkin' about mad wi' eggs'. She said she must have been swallowing them without realizing how many she had already had. Finally the 'vice' had come up to her and said she'd to go home. She'd been so out of control she'd just walked a big circle and bumped into them again and this time they demanded she go and get a taxi 'but I couldnae, I hadnae done a thing all night, I don't know how I got up the road, I cannae remember a thing'.

> Alice said that women who come down to work all jellied up [heavily under the influence of temazepam] rarely make any money. 'They'll go to you, "Did I do any work yesterday?" and you'll go, "Aye, you were in and out of motors all night." So when they say, "How come I've nae money now?" you have to say, "Because you got robbed." I mean I've seen birds robbing birds that's full of jellies.'

It was clear from our interviews that on the whole the clients were trying to avoid women who were injecting drugs. On the basis of our data, the likelihood of a client being successful in this respect is slim. The reason for this is not simply the sheer number of women working who were injecting drugs, but because, with the exception of those women who were very obviously experiencing the effects of recent drug use, most of the women were very capable at concealing their drug use from clients:

> A guy I brought up here the other night he asked me [about drugs]. I was walking back to the bedroom and ma shorts were off and there were all bruises on ma legs. He says, 'Do you take drugs?' I was doin' a hand job and I said, 'No,' and he says, 'What happened to your arms then?' I just said, 'I don't want to talk about it,' and he was like, 'Why what happened?' and I was like that [looks embarrassed], 'somebody battered me right.' And he said, 'Oh I'm sorry, I'm sorry.'

Other women, though more forceful, were equally adept at dealing with clients' attempts at finding out whether they were injecting drugs:

> The guy said to me, 'Can I see your arms?' 'No you cannae see ma arms, do ye no' believe me, all ye have to dae is start your car up and take me back

where ye got me.' 'I believe you, I believe you, I'm very sorry for putting you in that position,' he says.

Needle and syringe sharing among the women

Our information on whether the women were sharing injecting equipment is hampered to an extent by the fact that we were providing women with injecting equipment. This is very likely to have resulted in some women wanting to conceal any needle sharing from us. Despite this there clearly were occasions in our fieldwork where sharing did occur among the women:

> Frances came running over to us for some needles. She was clearly relieved at being able to get some as she said 'I'm needin' needles, we've all been diggin' intae the one set.' At this point she trailed off, not wanting to say any more about it.

> We met up with two women working who were sisters, one of them had been married a week. Both were injecting drugs, heroin mostly. They had hit up an hour ago and shared needles then. This was not because they didn't have needles since we'd met them at the beginning of the evening and they'd just been to the drop-in and taken supplies of clean needles and syringes. The one I spoke to said she'd used her sister's needle and that she'd also shared with her boyfriend. Her sister told Neil that she'd passed on her needle to her sister but didn't share with her although she would use her husband's.

In another case, it seems very likely that needles would have been shared had the woman not contacted and taken needles from us:

> Two of the women were away to get their hits and saw us. As we passed, one shouted out, 'I've been lookin' for you two, I'm away to get a hit but I've nae needles. I've got sets in the house but nothing down here. Ma pal says he could get me his sister's set to borrow but I can get some off you now.'

Taylor *et al.* (1993) have reported data on needle and syringe sharing among a small sample of Glasgow prostitutes who were opportunistically included in a larger study of drug-injectors in Glasgow. They found that 45 per cent ($n = 51$) of the women injected with used needles in the last six months although the majority of this was reported as having been with the women's sexual partners. Needle sharing was undoubtedly occurring among the women even if we are unable to identify the frequency with which it was taking place. That said, it is also the case that the provision of clean injecting equipment by the prostitute drop-in has done much to reduce the incidence of sharing since needle availability in the immediate area has been much improved:

> A young woman we met up with said she'd been really hoping to see us the night before. 'By the time I got down here the drop-in was shut so I was lookin' around for youse two but I didnae get you. In the end I asked one of the other lassies to gie me a set.' I asked if this had been a clean needle. 'No,

she jus' gave me one of hers she'd got in the drop-in. I don't think there's much sharing goes on down here now 'cos someone's always got extra sets of clean works.'

Conclusion

In this chapter we have described the influence which injecting drug use had on the street prostitution scene in Glasgow. It may well be that the extent of the overlap between injecting drug use and prostitution is greater in Glasgow than in any other UK city. However, we will really only know that if there are similar studies conducted in other cities using the same method of identifying whether the women are injecting. The extent of the overlap between prostitution and injecting drug use in Glasgow must give some cause for concern and indicates the importance of providing services to the women which respond to the multiple problems associated with an injecting lifestyle (Green *et al.* 1994).

It was often alleged by the non-injecting women that most of the unprotected sex occurring within the red-light area, as well as most of the theft from clients, involved those women who were working to finance a drug habit. There is clearly no way of resolving this issue. Having said this it has to be recognized that some of the most desperate women working in the area were those who were maintaining their own and, very often, their partner's drug habit. Where a woman is experiencing the unpleasant effects of drug withdrawal on a night when there are few clients around it is difficult to see how she might not be tempted to comply with a client's request for unprotected sex or to take advantage of other opportunities for obtaining money.

In the next chapter we shift our attention from the women selling sex to the men buying sex.

4

Buying sex: the views
of the clients

Introduction

To say that the clients of female prostitutes are a shadowy lot would be an
understatement. For the most part men buying sex remain invisible – their
features only becoming apparent when a celebrity's dalliance hits the
headlines. At the time of writing, the latest case to hit the news-stands is that of
the actor Hugh Grant, star of the film *Four Weddings and a Funeral*. Newspapers
and television alike are posing the same questions – why do men who are in
stable relationships buy sex? Why would a wealthy, good-looking and well
connected man buy sex on the streets? Should the female partners of such men
stand by them in the full glare of public scrutiny or should they summarily send
them packing?

   Despite the obvious interest in such questions in the press and elsewhere, in
fact we know very little about men buying sex. Over the last few years there
has been an explosion of publications, both academic and popular, looking at
various aspects of prostitution, but the focus in the vast majority of these is on
the women selling sex rather than the men out there buying sex. The reasons
for this are not hard to find. As we found out in our own research, men buying
sex are very reluctant to reveal who they are and talk openly about their
activities. One of the clients we interviewed said to us that he had 'never' told
anybody that he had paid for sex – 'After all,' he added, 'you never know how
they are going to react.'

   Although there is considerable interest in men paying for sex there are few
studies that allow us to estimate how many men actually do buy sex. In a
national study of sexual attitudes and lifestyles carried out in over 19,000
households in the UK, 1.8 per cent of men reported having paid for sex in the
last five years (Johnson *et al.* 1994). In contrast a national telephone survey of
Swiss males estimated that 12 per cent of men aged between 17 and 30 had

Table 4   Background characteristics of client sample

	Genito-urinary medicine group (n = 68)	Non-clinic group (n = 75)	Total (n = 143)
Mean age (years) (range in brackets)	36.8 (21–60)	35.2 (23–63)	36 (21–63)
Unemployed (percentage in brackets)	10 (15)	6 (8)	16 (11)
Married/cohabiting (percentage in brackets)	23 (34)	49 (65)	72 (50)
Past history of sexually transmitted infection (percentage in brackets)	31 (46)	4 (5)	35 (24)
Tested for HIV (percentage in brackets)	31 (46)	12 (16)	43 (30)

paid for sex (Hausser *et al.* 1991). A study of the sexual behaviour of over 2000 Dutch military personnel on detachment in Cambodia during June 1992 revealed that 45 per cent had had sexual contact with prostitutes or the local population (Buma *et al.* 1995). A study carried out in Lisbon found that out of 200 men surveyed 25 per cent had begun their sexual life on the basis of contact with a prostitute (Amaro *et al.* 1995). It is clearly not possible to make general statements about the number of men buying sex on the basis of these studies. Nevertheless it would appear that a significant number of men are paying for sex and further that this varies enormously across different areas.

In this chapter we look not so much at the number of men buying sex but at their views and experiences of prostitution. We look here at the kinds of sex they were buying, the appeal of paid sex, what they looked for in a prostitute and their fears in relation to HIV. We also look at the men's views as to how they thought their partners might react if they found out about their contacts with female prostitutes. We begin by presenting some of the quantitative information on the different kinds of sex the men were purchasing and then look more at their views and experiences.

In total we managed to interview 143 clients of prostitutes. About half were interviewed on the telephone (68 men). These were responding to an advertisement placed in a national tabloid. The other half were recruited and interviewed in a genito-urinary clinic (66 men). As we indicated in Chapter 1, trying to interview men on the streets proved extremely difficult; however, we did manage to recruit nine men in this manner (Barnard *et al.* 1993).

In Table 4 we have summarized some of the background characteristics of the men we interviewed. From this table we see that most of the men were employed; 50 per cent of them were either married or otherwise living with their partner. Although nearly a third of the men had been HIV tested it is notable that the majority were from the genito-urinary clinic sample. Whether this had anything to do with the men's prostitute contacts is impossible to say.

Most of the men reported having paid for vaginal sex; 89 had paid for masturbation or other non-penetrative sex and 87 had paid for oral sex. Eleven men said that they had paid for anal sex. In terms of condom use, 17 men said that they had not used a condom on the last occasion when they had purchased vaginal sex and 31 men said that they had not used a condom on the last occasion of buying oral sex. All of the cases of anal sex were, according to the men, protected. Of those men who reported using a condom when they had last paid for sex, 14 per cent stated that the condom had burst. This last figure is important because it reminds us that while condoms reduce the risk of HIV and other sexually transmitted infections, they do not eliminate it. As a result both clients and prostitutes remain at some risk even where condoms are used (de Graaf 1995).

Establishing accurate information on levels of condom use reported by the clients was no more straightforward for the men than for the women and requires some interpretation rather than the simple presentation of reported levels. The clients we interviewed were not reporting universal condom use with prostitutes. We should not, however, take these figures at face value. In much the same way that some of the women may have been denying providing unprotected sex, some of the clients may have been falsely claiming to have purchased unprotected sex. The reasons for this are likely to be complex and have to do with the men's views of their own power over prostitute women and their desires regarding such women. Some of the men we interviewed, for example, stated that they were in charge of the encounter with the prostitute and that the satisfaction of their needs and desires was uppermost in determining what happened with the prostitute. Such men may then have been reluctant to grant that a prostitute had successfully insisted on a condom being used if that was not their own personal preference. It seems likely that the true level of condom use between prostitutes and clients in our study rests some way between the reports of universal use provided by the women and the intermittent use claimed by the men.

The information on the kinds of sex purchased and whether it was protected tells us little about the attraction of paid sex for the men. In the remainder of the chapter we look at some of the qualitative information from our interviews.

The attraction of paid sex

In describing the appeal of sex with a prostitute the clients drew attention to five aspects which were felt to be important. These were the capacity to specify particular sex acts they wished to perform, or have performed on them; the capacity to have sex with a range of different women; the ability to seek out women with specific physical attributes or displaying particular images; the thrill of doing something that was socially frowned upon; and the limited and unemotional nature of the contact with the prostitute. We illustrate the kinds of things the men said about each of these below.

Specific sexual acts

Many of the men drew attention to the fact that they felt it was much easier to ask a prostitute to do certain things than their sexual partner. This was also cited as a reason for visiting prostitutes by many of the clients interviewed in a London study (Day *et al*. 1993). Very often reference would be made to oral sex or to different sexual positions:

> What do I like about sex with a prostitute? The fact of being able to get oral, with or without a condom to the point of coming in her mouth.

> My wife is not very interested in anything other than straight sex and with a prostitute the world is your oyster.

> Anal, I've only done that once with a prostitute, but it's perhaps more difficult to ask a girlfriend to do. Also I quite enjoy dressing up in ladies' underwear which again I would not ask a partner to do.

Other men described buying what they described as 'specialist sexual services' which included such things as whipping, bondage and various forms of physical degradation including being urinated and defecated upon.

There was an interesting distinction in the way in which the clients would explain their purchasing of these various acts. Those men who were buying oral or vaginal sex would sometimes explain their reasons for doing so by citing a reluctance on the part of their partner to participate in such acts. In the case of the specialist sexual services, by contrast, there appeared to be much less of an expectation from the men that their own partners would provide such services:

> He said he was at ease with prostitutes, he could 'indulge in things which you couldn't indulge in with other women'. In particular he mentioned that it would be difficult to get a woman to agree to corporal punishment which is what he likes to have done to him.

One client who said that he had managed to persuade his partner to whip him explained that the whipping he had then received had been carried out with such an obvious lack of enthusiasm that he resolved thereafter to confine his requests for various forms of punishment to his prostitute contacts.

Different women

For some men the appeal of sex with a prostitute seemed to have less to do with their wish to buy specific sexual acts than with the opportunity to have sex with a large number of different women. Some men drew attention to the fact that before they were married they had been sexually involved with large numbers of women and they wished to continue this without the complications of maintaining a fully fledged affair or series of affairs:

I used to have different partners before I met my wife and it's just something I missed. To me it's better to do it this way than to go to a night-club, pick up a girl, go back to her place or do it in a car and end up catching something.

Other men, by contrast, stressed that for a variety of reasons, including concerns about HIV, they limited their prostitute contacts to specific women. Indeed one of the clients we interviewed had been paying for sex from the same woman for longer than the thirteen years he had been married to his wife.

Specific physical characteristics

Prostitution also offered the men the opportunity to have sex with specific types of women. Attention would be drawn, for example, to women of a certain age or ethnic background, or to women who had a certain look whether tarty, strict, or prim and proper:

I always look for a woman who is young, shapely, not too busty.

You wouldn't believe this but it is the little things, like she's got to have long legs or she looks a bit of a bitch. If she stands there and looks really nice that would be a complete turn-off, she's got to look a bit bitchy, a bit of a tart.

Age is important. I like them as young as I can find them, 16 is the youngest I've had them, early 20s, beyond that I'm not interested. I'm 40 now and I just prefer them younger.

The woman I see at the moment is a coloured girl and there aren't many coloured girls round here so I stick with her.

Limited nature of the contact

Apart from the actual sex involved it was clear from our interviews that many men were attracted by the uninvolved nature of the contact with the prostitute:

The attractions of prostitutes are that it's easy. We both know what we want, there's no charade. If I go to a club or something I have to work for it but with a prostitute it's pure sex, no-one's kidding the other.

It was just the fact that here were women who would do anything, you know that was required, no bones about it plus the fact that there was no commitment at all. You know, it was for a specific purpose that you became involved, then it was over and you could go back to work. If you wanted another one it was just a matter of going along making your choice and so on.

It is interesting to note that the image of the prostitute which these men held was very much at odds with that articulated by the women. Far from describing themselves as prepared to 'do anything' most of the women we interviewed stressed that they were in charge of the contact with the clients, that they limited the sexual services they would provide and that they decided what would and what would not happen.

The clandestine nature of the contact

Finally, it was clear that some clients in this study, as well as some interviewed in a North American study (Holzman and Pines 1982), viewed the illicit nature of buying sex from a prostitute as itself a source of enjoyment:

> It's difficult to say what the attraction is, I think to a certain amount it's the dare of doing it and of being able to do things that you couldn't do with your wife.

> It's the thrill of it being illicit, unknown and the fact that you can be a bit more adventurous.

The clients' views of prostitute women

As the men talked about their contact with women selling sex, they repeatedly stressed the attraction of a woman whom one could ask to do anything. In part this feeling seemed to be rooted in the clients' belief that because they had the money so they had the power over the prostitute:

> It's easier to ask a prostitute to do things because she's there to service you, you know you're paying her for the service. It's like going to have your car done, you tell them what you want done, they don't ask, you tell them you want so and so done and if they don't do it, fair enough, you go down the road to someone else.

The feeling of being able to ask for anything was about more than money. In the mind's eye of many, if not most, of the clients, the prostitute seemed to be no more than the sex she sold. Whether the prostitute had a view on the sex she was being asked to provide was not so much unknown as irrelevant. In the men's view, the prostitute was there to provide sex, not to comment on it.

To some clients the fact of having paid for sex conferred a certain power over the women. We saw in the previous chapter how the women would describe themselves as being in charge of the encounter with the client – it was clear from the client interviews that they also felt that they were in charge of the encounter. As one client put it, 'you've got a bit more dominance, you've got the money in your pocket, then you've got the dominance over them'. Having said this there were clients who talked about 'value for money', who recognized that once the act was over, they had limited redress if they felt they had not had a very satisfactory experience:

> Like there'll be a difference between what they promised and what they delivered and you go away feeling disappointed. I mean your bargaining power's limited in that situation. You're on known territory and with your

trousers down. You can't really say, well, that wasn't good enough once it's over, you can't really demand your money back can you?

It is not difficult to see why the prostitute/client relationship itself should have been so potentially volatile. In many respects the prostitutes and clients held divergent views on the sexual encounter, at the heart of which was the issue of power and control. We discuss one of the expressions of that volatility, the violence which was associated with the women's work, in Chapter 6. A clear sense of the manoeuvring for power in the prostitute/client encounter can be gleaned from a client who describes looking for the prostitute whom he feels he will be most able to control:

> After being there a few times what you start looking for is the newcomer rather than the woman that you know that you saw last week and last month, yes the newcomer who is perhaps not so businesslike about things you like, they tend to be a bit more amenable to your requests, whereas for the older hands at the game anything is extra, everything is extra.

It is interesting to see how the financial nature of the transaction has an uncertain status in this client's view. The fact that the 'old hand' prostitute will charge for any extras, whereas the new women may be too naïve to do so, is not simply about saving money but also the desirability of concealing the true nature of the transaction. The client knows that his sex with the prostitute is a financial matter but he does not appear to want that reality to permeate the entire encounter with the prostitute.

Clients and HIV infection

The encounters between prostitutes and their clients were carried out against the backdrop of HIV infection. Almost all of the men we interviewed expressed concern about HIV; however, it should be borne in mind that about half of the sample were recruited from a sexually transmitted diseases clinic and might therefore be expected to be more acutely aware of their own risks in relation to HIV.

We asked the clients for their own estimates of the extent of HIV infection among prostitutes in their local area. On average the men suggested that 33 per cent of the women would be HIV positive, although some men estimated the figure to be as high as 70 or 80 per cent. The actual extent of HIV among prostitute women is considered in Chapter 5. It is sufficient to say here that levels of HIV infection among female prostitutes have rarely been shown to exceed 5 per cent in developed countries. The clients we interviewed were holding wildly exaggerated beliefs about the extent of HIV infection among working women. Indeed, in their own estimates, many of these men were placing themselves in the centre of an HIV epidemic the like of which has only been recorded in parts of Africa. Yet despite this they were still buying sex. Clearly, if anyone thought that HIV/AIDS might signal the end of prostitution, they would be wrong.

Despite the fact that many of these men believed HIV was very common among prostitute women, hardly any of them felt that they were personally at risk of infection as a result of their prostitute contacts. It is interesting to consider the basis for the clients' optimism in this respect. First, the men believed that although HIV was common among prostitute women it was concentrated among women working on the streets. By contacting women working in off-street locations the risks, in their minds, were significantly reduced:

> I wouldn't touch them on the streets because I find that most of them on the streets are injecting.

> I tend to look at their arms very carefully as quick as I can. If I felt that any of them were drug users I wouldn't touch them. Obviously you can't always tell but you get a feeling from talking to people.

It was clear from these and similar comments that in trying to recognize women injecting drugs the men were very much thinking in terms of an 'addict stereotype': track marks, abscesses, vacant expression, etc. As we pointed out in Chapter 3, many of the women we interviewed who were injecting would never have been recognizable from such external signs.

Clients also made judgements about the level of risk which different women might represent in terms of their general appearance, how much the women charged, whether they washed themselves between clients, and even on their method of contacting clients:

> I have some regular women that I have known for a number of years. There's another one and she does not even advertise herself, she's got a flat and a known number of people who contact her. She sticks to the people that have her telephone number, you go and visit her if she's available, sometimes she's not available but that's how she operates, doesn't make any further new contacts.

> I wouldn't have thought any of the ones I've been with are drug users. I think if you look at some people you can tell. I mean I suppose they have injection marks on their arms and what have you, I think they also tend to be the dirtier scruffier types. I would rather pay more and go with someone who I thought was a bit cleaner. Like the girl I go with now, I know for a fact that she showers between, like, seeing me and someone else.

Some of the men we interviewed stated that were it not for the fact of always using a condom with their prostitute contacts they believed they would be at considerable risk of HIV:

> Let's put it this way, if I wasn't using a condom, my risks of HIV would be very high. Even with a condom I suppose I have to be very careful to check that it has not burst and that I don't do anything without a condom.

> I always use a condom. To me to ask for sex without is an insult, it is saying to her 'I think you are dirty enough to have it without'.

As we noted earlier in this chapter a significant minority of men reported not having used a condom for vaginal and oral sex involving a prostitute. With the exception of their use of condoms, the main methods these clients were using to reduce their risks (basically that of trying to avoid those women whom they thought posed the greatest risk) were simply inadequate to the task at hand.

Informing others

Many of the articles on prostitution in the popular and quality press have expressed concern, not for the prostitute or her client, but for the risks facing the client's sexual partner and children of contracting a sexually transmitted disease, particularly HIV. It is difficult to quantify the actual level of additional risk faced by partners as a result of their husbands or boyfriends buying sex from a prostitute. What is beyond question, however, is the fact that without knowing about such contacts, no woman is in a position to protect herself against such risk. The question which follows on from this is, how many of the men we were interviewing had told their partner about their contact with a prostitute?

It will come as no surprise that hardly any of the men had informed their partner of their sexual contacts with prostitutes. The assumption among the men was that their prostitute contacts and relationships with private partners existed within quite separate spheres of their life. One man who had informed his sexual partner about a past contact with a prostitute said that she had become so concerned that she had asked him to be tested for HIV. Another client had accompanied his wife on a visit to her doctor to discuss a gynaecological problem she had been experiencing for some time. He had sat in the waiting room silently rehearsing how he was going to tell his wife about his prostitute contact, believing that this must have been the cause of her infection. The doctor's diagnosis of the problem had, he pointed out, saved him from the need to reveal the knowledge to his wife. Finally, another client stated that his wife must have known about his paying a prostitute to whip him because he felt certain that she had seen the scars on his body. Both of them, he believed, had silently agreed not to talk about the matter further and had never done so.

In addition to asking the men whether they had informed their partner about their prostitute contacts we also asked them what they thought their partner's reaction would be to being provided with such information. The consensus among all of the men we interviewed was that such information would have a disastrous impact on their relationship:

> If I told my wife she'd kick me out, simple as that.

> The reaction of my wife if I told her; she'd be hurt, horrified, she wouldn't understand and it would probably end our marriage.

> For me it's completely separate. I'd never tell my partner – you just don't do that. In fact not only wouldn't I tell my partner, I wouldn't tell anybody.

> If I told her she'd be horrified.

These were the kinds of reactions which the men anticipated. It is possible of course that they may have been very wrong in their judgements in this respect.

Nevertheless the consensus among the men was that imparting the knowledge of having paid for sex would be so destructive as to rule it out as an option. A number of the men even pointed out that they felt it would be easier to tell their partner about a longstanding affair than to reveal their prostitute contacts.

In some ways it is rather odd that the clients should anticipate any similarity in the reaction of their partner between a fleeting and emotionally uninvolved contact with a prostitute and a longstanding affair. That a parallel should be drawn between these two tells us a good deal about the ambiguities which surround sex in general and prostitution in particular. One of the reasons why the knowledge that one's partner has paid for sex may be so destructive is the assumption, which many of us make, that we should be able to meet our partner's sexual needs. The fact that one's partner has sought sexual gratification elsewhere can be sufficient to invoke a deep sense of uncertainty about our own ability to contribute fully to the relationship. Further, the fact that sex has been bought may be interpreted as a sign that sex for one's partner has become devoid of emotional content. It is an open question whether it is better to perform an act which our partner requests but from which we derive no pleasure, and which may even be offensive, or to accept that the act can and will be purchased elsewhere. Whichever option one might choose, a necessary precondition to such a decision would seem to be the ability to openly discuss both one's own and one's partner's sexual needs. It is ironic that many of the men we interviewed only felt able to enter into such a discussion, at least regarding their own sexual needs, once the relationship with the woman had acquired a financial basis.

This chapter has afforded us no more than a glimpse into the world of the clients, their views of the prostitutes they were paying for sex and the kinds of sex they were buying. In a sense there is nothing particularly dramatic in the views which these men expressed or the requests which most of them were making. This is not surprising since the drama associated with exchanging sex for money exists not so much in what is bought and sold (after all any sex is really only a variation on a theme) but in our attitudes towards prostitution itself and those it encompasses.

In the next chapter we shift our focus somewhat and look at what is known about the link between prostitution and AIDS.

5

Prostitution and HIV/AIDS

Introduction

As with so many aspects of our public and private lives, a distinction can be drawn between prostitution before AIDS was known about and the situation now. In the time before HIV and AIDS were discovered, prostitutes were frequently represented as vectors of syphilis and other sexually transmitted diseases, particularly in the early years of the twentieth century (Roberts 1992). Serious as the threat was seen to be at the time, it receded considerably with the advent of powerful antibiotic drugs. With the advent of HIV/AIDS the wheel has turned full circle and prostitutes are back on the public health agenda, this time charged with spreading HIV infection. One does not need to scratch too far below the surface of many reports on the links between prostitution and HIV to recognize that the true object of concern is frequently not prostitutes themselves but heterosexual society symbolized in the 'innocent victims' – clients' wives, girlfriends and children.

Prostitution and AIDS make a volatile mix, combining our interest in sex with our fear of illness and death. It is a mix which has generated a great deal of heat and relatively little light. In this chapter we will cut through some of the headline froth to look at what is actually known about the links between HIV/AIDS and prostitution. We look first at the results of those studies which have tried to identify the extent of HIV infection among female prostitutes in different parts of the world. We then look at what is known about the extent of condom use between prostitutes and their clients as well as with their private partners.

The prevalence of HIV infection among female prostitutes

It is immediately apparent from looking at the results of those studies reporting levels of HIV among prostitute women that there is no one pattern of HIV

Table 5   Female prostitution and HIV infection (areas of high prevalence)

Country/city	Sample	% HIV positive	Author	Date
Nairobi	418	62	Simonsen *et al.*	1990
Yaounde	262	45.3	Monny-Lube *et al.*	1993
Nairobi	2162	44	Kitabu *et al.*	1992
Kinshasa	1233	35	Nzila *et al.*	1991
Douala	234	26.6	Monny-Lube *et al.*	1993
Thailand	825	44.6	Chaisiri *et al.*	1993
North Thailand	76	38	Mastro *et al.*	1993
Chiangmai	238	36.5	Siraprapasiri *et al.*	1991
Bombay	451	36	Bhave *et al.*	1992
Thailand	797	22	Tirasawat *et al.*	1993
New York	583	27.8	Hoffman *et al.*	1992
Miami	359	26	Onorato *et al.*	1992
Puerto Rico	176	25	Vera *et al.*	1992

Table 6   Female prostitution and HIV infection (areas of medium prevalence)

Country/city	Sample	% HIV positive	Author	Date
Lagos	693	12	Dada *et al.*	1993
Spain	1665	12.5	Estébanez *et al.*	1992
Montreal	907	11.4	Lamothe *et al.*	1993
Rio de Janeiro	69	11.6	De Meis *et al.*	1991
Buenos Aires	178	11.6	Multare *et al.*	1992
São Paulo	600	11	Fernandes *et al.*	1992

spread between prostitutes and their clients. The picture is different depending on where in the world one looks.

Some of the highest levels of infection recorded anywhere in the world have been found in studies of female prostitutes in Africa. The African continent itself, however, is an area with widely differing rates of infection both within and between different countries. To emphasize the point that HIV infection levels are geographically variable, even within parts of the same land mass, Tables 5, 6 and 7 show figures for areas of high, medium and low prevalence.

The high level of HIV infection identified in a number of these studies is not simply a reflection of very high levels of infection within the general population. In Nairobi, Kenya, for example, 44 per cent of 2162 female prostitutes were found to be HIV positive in 1991 whilst only 17.2 per cent of 5033 pregnant women tested over the same period were found to be HIV positive (Kitabu *et al.* 1992).

In addition to identifying high levels of HIV infection, a number of these studies have also found high levels of other sexually transmitted infections among prostituting women. In the Nairobi study, for example, 28 per cent of

Table 7 Female prostitution and HIV infection (areas of low prevalence)

Country/city	Sample	% HIV positive	Author	Date
Côte d'Ivoire	278	9.2	Traore-Ettiegne *et al.*	1993
Zaire	1161	7.3	Delaporte *et al.*	1992
Gambia	–	7	Pepin *et al.*	1991
Dakar	3375	4.3	Wade *et al.*	1993
Somalia	548	2.1	Corwin *et al.*	1991
Sierra Leone	11,750	0.9	Kosia *et al.*	1993
Calcutta	450	1.1	Jana *et al.*	1993
Sri Lanka	253	0	Samarakoon	1993
Japan	191	0	Kihara *et al.*	1993
Denmark	29,708	9.1	Smith *et al.*	1993
Vancouver	636	8	Rekart	1993
United States	1305	7	Khabbaz *et al.*	1990
Europe	866	4.8	European Working Group	1993
Glasgow	165	3.6	Carr *et al.*	1992
Los Angeles County	638	2.5	Kanouse *et al.*	1992
Glasgow	156	2.5	McKeganey *et al.*	1992
Spain	678	2.3	Pineda *et al.*	1992
London	280	0.9	Ward *et al.*	1993
Copenhagen	207	0	Alary and Worm	1993
Buenos Aires	237	6.3	Zapiola *et al.*	1992
Uruguay	2500	5.6	Somma *et al.*	1993
Argentina	362	3	Fay *et al.*	1992
Nicaragua	130	0.8	Espinoza *et al.*	1993
Mexico	17,184	0.5	Valdespino *et al.*	1992

the women had genital ulcers and 32 per cent had laboratory-diagnosed evidence of syphilis (Simonsen *et al.* 1990). The importance of this information is highlighted by the fact that a number of studies have shown that the presence of other sexually transmitted infections (especially if they involve genital ulcers) can substantially increase the risk of contracting HIV infection (Aral 1993).

No less important than the information on the overall extent of HIV infection among prostitute women are the reported rates at which new cases are occurring; such incidence data are important because they provide an indication of the rate at which the epidemic is spreading within a given area. Some of the studies which have been carried out in the high HIV prevalence areas have suggested that the rate of new infections may be as high as 50 per cent per year. Indeed one study has suggested that, given the levels of HIV infection identified within some of these areas, it is remarkable that any of those prostitutes not using condoms consistently remain HIV negative (Simonsen *et al.* 1990). There has been some speculation that the reason why some women have remained HIV negative, despite intense exposure to HIV through prostitution, might indicate the acquisition or natural development of a kind of resistance to HIV infection (Fowke *et al.* 1992).

If Africa has seen some of the highest recorded levels of HIV among prostitute women, it has also seen some of the lowest. For example, in Somalia, only 2.1 per cent of 548 prostitutes tested were found to be HIV positive (Corwin *et al.* 1991). Whether some of the low HIV prevalence areas will develop an increasing HIV problem over time is not at all clear. What is known, however, is that there is a good deal of geographical mobility between women working in different countries (Pickering *et al.* 1992). The possibility of more extensive spread, although possibly at a slower rate, can therefore hardly be discounted.

The only other part of the world which seems to be experiencing an epidemic of HIV on a par with that identified in parts of Africa is Asia. There has been a good deal of media attention focused upon the sex industry in Thailand, which has faced an explosion of HIV infection in the last few years. Some of the highest levels of infection have been recorded in the northern parts of the country as well as among women serving lower-class clients (Siraprapasiri *et al.* 1991). The finding that prostitutes from lower socio-economic groups in Thailand have higher levels of HIV infection than prostitutes from higher socio-economic groups parallels the situation found in a number of the African countries. It illustrates very well how poverty can further compound the tragedy of widespread infection such that the poorest sections of society are those hardest hit. This latter fact is of course not confined to Africa or Asia but is equally well demonstrated in studies carried out in the United States where some of the highest levels of HIV infection have been identified among black and Hispanic inner city populations.

Although widespread among female prostitutes in Thailand, HIV is not confined to that country. HIV has also been identified in female prostitutes in other parts of Asia, for example, Bombay, India (Bhave *et al.* 1992). However, even in those countries where low levels of infection have been recorded to date, high levels of other sexually transmitted infections have sometimes been recorded, illustrating the potential for HIV spread within those areas. In Sri Lanka, for example, out of 253 female prostitutes tested, none were found to be HIV positive; however, 72 per cent of the women had at least one sexually transmitted infection (Samarakoon, 1993).

The rate at which HIV is spreading among prostitutes within some of the Asian countries is just as worrying as the overall level of infection identified. Once again most concern to date has centred on Thailand. One study of 100 female prostitutes, tested in 1989, found 44 women who were HIV positive. A second study carried out two months later found that 20 per cent of the women who had been HIV negative in the first study had become HIV positive, suggesting a rate of new cases of around 10 per cent per month – a doubling of the total every ten months (Siraprapasiri *et al.* 1991).

Throughout Europe, Australia and North America, HIV infection among female prostitutes is really a tale of not one epidemic but two – one among those prostitutes injecting drugs and one among prostitutes who do not inject. One of the largest studies ever conducted among female prostitutes was carried out in nine European centres and involved studying 866 women. Of this total, 42 women were found to be HIV positive, suggesting an overall HIV prevalence rate for female prostitutes in Europe of around 4.8 per cent (European

Working Group 1993). The impact of injecting drug use on rates of HIV infection among prostitute women is dramatic. In Spain, for example, 3.4 per cent of non-injecting female prostitutes were found to be HIV positive whereas the figure leapt to 50.9 per cent in the case of those women who were injecting drugs (Estébanez *et al.* 1992). By contrast, a study by Pineda and colleagues (1992) found no evidence of an increase in HIV infection among non-drug-injecting prostitutes in Spain.

This clustering of cases of HIV infection among those prostitutes injecting drugs has also been found in studies carried out in Australia (Harcourt and Philpot 1990; Philpot *et al.* 1991) and France (De Vincenzi *et al.* 1992) as well as the United Kingdom (McKeganey *et al.* 1992; Ward *et al.* 1993) and the United States (Khabbaz *et al.* 1990). In New York City, out of 583 street prostitutes tested in 1991, 27.8 per cent were found to be HIV positive. In the case of those women injecting drugs, however, 60 per cent were found to be HIV positive (Hoffman *et al.* 1992).

In the United States, Khabbaz and colleagues (1990) have estimated that around 7.0 per cent of female prostitutes might be HIV positive. This figure though masks what in reality are large differences between parts of the US. In Los Angeles, where HIV is low among injecting drug users, only 2.5 per cent of more than 600 female street working prostitutes tested were found to be HIV positive (Kanouse *et al.* 1992). In New York city by contrast, 27.8 per cent of 583 female street working prostitutes were found to be HIV positive (Hoffman *et al.* 1992). In the case of those women injecting drugs the figure is even higher – 60 per cent. In Miami 26 per cent of over 300 women tested in 1990 were found to be HIV positive. The researchers on this study were also able to show that there had been a dramatic increase in the rate of new HIV infections from an estimated 3.0 per cent per 100 person years in 1987 to 14.7 per cent in 1991. The authors of this report conclude that within Miami, female sex workers are at great risk of acquiring HIV infection (Onorato *et al.* 1992).

Many of the US studies have identified high levels of other sexually transmitted diseases among female prostitutes; 47 per cent of over 600 women tested in Los Angeles county, for example, reported one or more sexually transmitted infection in the last six months (Kanouse *et al.* 1992). In a large study of over 1300 female prostitutes recruited from across the US, Rosenblum and colleagues found that 56 per cent of the women had evidence of past or present hepatitis infection. This figure rose to 74 per cent in the case of those women who were prostituting and injecting drugs (1992).

If one recalls the views expressed by many of the clients we interviewed, that women injecting drugs posed the greatest risk, we can see, on the basis of these figures, that, to an extent, the clients were correct. Where they were plainly incorrect, however, was in believing that they could recognize those women who were injecting. There is a further point to make here concerning the issue of whether women working on the streets are more likely to be HIV positive than women working in off-street locations such as bars, clubs, brothels or escort agencies. Despite the fact that many clients appeared to believe that this was the case, there is simply not enough information available on women working in off-street prostitution to be confident of the assertion that HIV is clustered among women working on the streets.

Within parts of the United States, the use of crack cocaine appears to have had a major impact on levels of HIV infection among female prostitutes. There is evidence that the use of crack not only increases the likelihood of a woman prostituting, but also of her being HIV positive. In a study of 789 ante-natal patients in the United States 5.3 per cent of the women reported using crack and, of these women, 26 per cent were found to be HIV positive compared to only 2 per cent of the non-crack-users. Before using crack, 17 per cent of the drug users in this study reported having worked as a prostitute, while among the crack users 72 per cent reported having engaged in such work (Schoenfisch *et al.* 1993).

The potential for HIV spread associated with sexual activity taking place within crack houses has been vividly portrayed in qualitative interviews with crack users:

> I really didn't think much about it [HIV]. I was high, and I had been high most of the night and parking [having vaginal intercourse with] a crack house prostitute while she was on the rag [menstruating] was something I had done more than once in my time. . . . She was bleeding and I was bleeding, first from a bad blow job and then from too much sex. . . . After a while the blood, hers, got too much so I turned her over and put it in her chute [anus].

(Quoted in Inciardi *et al.* 1993)

Use of crack cocaine has been associated with a marked increase in sexual activity and with a corresponding increase in the risk of sexual spread of HIV. It is worth stressing that the potential for such spread is not confined to those individuals who are involved in sex for money transactions but potentially all of those involved in crack-related sex.

On the basis of this brief review, the suggestion that HIV is commonplace among prostitute women is clearly a gross over-simplification. It is also factually incorrect for a number of countries. In *parts* of Africa and *parts* of Asia, HIV has been found to be widespread among female prostitutes. However, in other parts of both areas, HIV has not been shown to be prevalent among prostitute women. Within the developed world, HIV appears to be low among those female prostitutes who are not injecting drugs and a good deal higher in the case of those women who are doing so.

To judge the risks of HIV spread associated with female prostitution, we also need information on levels of condom use in prostitute/client contacts. There is a good deal of data on this from a variety of studies. Before looking at that data it is worth recognizing the difficulty of obtaining accurate information on the use or non-use of condoms. We have already presented some information on clients' self-reported condom use from our own study (see Chapter 4) and we have stressed some of the caveats in taking such reports at face value. Almost all of the research on condom use by prostitutes and clients is based upon individual self-report. For a variety of reasons, some of which we have outlined, these reports may not represent a complete correspondence with reality. One of the most interesting studies in this respect was carried out in Nicaragua and involved providing prostitutes with condoms as they were entering hotel rooms with clients. Once the prostitute and client had left, the researchers carried out a search of the room for any evidence that the condom had been used. In 85 per cent of cases they were able to retrieve the original condom; however, only 37 per cent of the recovered condoms contained semen and 48 per cent remained unopened (Gorter *et al.* 1993). In another notable study carried out in the Gambia, Pickering and colleagues interviewed both female prostitutes and clients as they were leaving the area where sex had been traded – in 22 per cent of almost 24,000 prostitute/client contacts there was disagreement between the two as to whether a condom had been used (Pickering *et al.* 1992). Both of these studies give an indication of the difficulty of establishing accurate information on such a private and hidden topic as condom use by prostitutes and their clients.

With this caveat in mind the broad picture that emerges from the available data is one of very high levels of condom use in those areas where low levels of HIV have been recorded and relatively low levels of condom use in some of those areas where very high levels of HIV infection have been identified. The European Working Group study, (prostitutes in this survey were based in Amsterdam, Antwerp, Athens, Lisbon, London, Madrid, Paris and Vienna) for example, have reported that 80.3 per cent of female prostitutes had always used condoms with clients in the previous six months. Researchers in Copenhagen (which has a very low HIV prevalence) found that 95 per cent of 237 prostitutes studied in the city were using condoms with clients (Alary *et al.* 1993) and in London 92.2 per cent of 304 female prostitutes studied were apparently consistently using condoms with clients (Ward *et al.* 1993). Near universal condom use by prostitutes has also been reported in Australia (Harcourt and Philpot 1990; Mulhall *et al.* 1995). In the United States, among 1024 street prostitutes studied between 1990 and 1991, only 12 per cent said that they had not used a condom on the last occasion of having provided vaginal sex, while 20 per cent reported non-use on the last occasion that they provided a client with oral sex (Berry *et al.* 1992).

In striking contrast to these figures showing very high levels of condom use, researchers in New Mexico found that just over half of the prostitute women they contacted were using condoms all of the time with clients (Tabet *et al.* 1992). Similarly, out of 1665 prostitutes studied in Spain between 1989 and 1991, only 35 per cent of women said that they always used condoms while working (Fitch *et al.* 1992). These latter figures are somewhat nearer the levels of reported condom use by prostitutes in parts of Africa and Asia.

In general, high levels of condom use between prostitutes and their clients are reported for many of the developed countries, but much lower levels of use have been reported for a number of the developing countries. A study carried out in Zaire, for example, found that of the 1233 prostitutes studied, 78 per cent of the women felt that they were at high risk of infection, although less than 15 per cent reported regularly using condoms with clients (Nzila *et al.* 1991). Similarly, in a study carried out in Nairobi of 103 men who had reported recently paying for sex, only 15 per cent said that they had used a condom on their last contact with a female prostitute (Otido *et al.* 1993). A study carried out among female prostitutes in Thailand found that of the 238 women surveyed, over half were using condoms intermittently with clients (Siraprapasiri *et al.* 1991). In the light of such figures there can be little doubt as to the potential for further HIV spread within many of the developing countries – both prostitutes and their clients are at considerable risk of HIV as a result of such low levels of condom use.

Factors influencing the non-use of condoms

Within the developing countries, the single greatest factor explaining the low levels of condom use is undoubtedly the relative lack of availability of condom supplies. In a study carried out in the Gambia, Pickering and colleagues found that in the early evening, rates of condom use by female prostitutes were high. By the late evening, as supplies diminished, their use was much less consistent (Pickering *et al.* 1993). Availability, not only of condom supplies, but of health care provision generally, remains a major problem within the developing countries.

Within the developed countries, as shown by evidence from Europe, North America and Australia, condom use with clients is reported as being very high. However, condom use with prostitutes' private partners has been shown to be very low. A number of reasons have been offered for this, including the concern on the part of prostitute women to maintain a clear distinction between sex for money and sex within the context of their private relationships – the condom acting as a symbol of that difference (Day 1988). It should also be remembered that many prostitute women will be involved in long-term relationships and that in choosing not to use condoms with their partners, they are actually making the same choice as most couples in longstanding heterosexual relationships.

Despite the very high levels of condom use with clients reported in many of the developed countries, their use still falls short of 100 per cent. In considering the possible reasons for this, what has to be discounted at the outset is the assumption that prostitutes are solely responsible for those occasions when condoms are not used. As we previously discussed, prostitute/client relationships, like relationships in general, incorporate issues to do with power. It might be possible for the prostitute to take control of the encounter nearly all of the time and, as part of this, insist on a condom being used. However there will, in all likelihood, be occasions where clients impose their own will on the prostitute, with or without threats of violence. On such occasions the client may insist that a condom is *not* used. The issue of power may very likely be a key factor in determining whether or not condoms are used. Within those societies where there is a cultural expectation of female passivity, prostitute women may feel unable to insist on condom use with clients, even where they themselves understand the risks of HIV and would prefer their client to use a condom. This was shown to be the case among female prostitutes working in Singapore, for example, where, although women understood the risks of HIV, nevertheless some of them felt unable to resist clients who were requesting unprotected sex (Wong *et al.* 1992, 1994). Expectations of female passivity are not solely to be found in distant and seemingly exotic cultures. Research on the sexual attitudes of males in many developed countries has shown similar expectations of female passivity and, correspondingly, male dominance. It would therefore be surprising if the issue of condom use did not similarly coalesce around notions of power and dominance.

The picture in terms of the women we interviewed was very much in accord with that reported in other studies elsewhere in Europe and North America – namely an expectation among the women that condoms should be used:

> I get in the car, in fact even before I get in I say it'll have to be with a condom, it's either yes or no, everything is with a condom.

> I've got a couple of punters who'll say I'll give you so and so if you'll do it without. But never, I always use a condom for anal sex, oral sex and even for hand jobs, there's no way I'll let them come anywhere near me.

However, such statements were often accompanied by the unproven assertion that there were, nevertheless, women working in the local area who were not using condoms:

> I know there are girls down here doing sex without a condom and that's just madness to me.

> If there wasnae women doing it without [a condom] what the hell are the punters asking us for? See that Tracey, she's going without. I've seen her with that wee Irishman who comes about here – he's always looking to do it without. I shouted down to her one day – 'Don't go with him' – but she just ignored me and had the cheek to bring him back and let him drop her off right in front of me. I shouted on at her, 'See wait a minute, what the fuck you doin', goin' with him without for?' But she ran off – if I'd have caught her I'd 'ave killed her. See that big fat Elise she goes without.

In addition to the reports of clients offering additional money for unprotected sex there were also reports of clients deliberately tearing condoms:

> I took the guy down there, I put the Durex on him and then I heard a noise ye make when the Durex comes off, but I felt the rim and it was there – but I kept thinking something's wrong. I could feel the bottom of it there, but as I went up, it felt different and what he'd done was, like, rip it off. I was dead, dead mad. I knew he'd meant it and he just said, 'Well give us another one then.'

There were also occasions in the fieldwork where it was clear that unprotected sex had been forcibly imposed upon women. This was usually in conjunction with situations where the client had raped the woman. The issue of violence is taken up more fully in the next chapter.

Many of the women we interviewed were frankly amazed that any client should still be requesting unprotected sex given the extensive coverage of the risks of HIV:

> You still get the bam-pots [idiots] asking for sex without. I had one the other night – I said, 'where have you been living – on a desert island?'

> If a punter's asking for sex without, then to me the only reason for that is he's probably got something himself.

He wanted me to do him a gam [oral] without a condom and swallow it. I said no I wouldnae do it, so then he offered me £15 if I did, but I still said no, I wouldnae. So then I shouted over to another lassie what he wanted and she said 'no' but when I said he'd pay £15 she said 'aye' and went away wi' him.

One reason why at least some clients may be requesting unprotected sex is the desire to do something to a prostitute that they believe no other client has been able to do. Certainly some of the men we interviewed seemed to want to remove the barrier which a condom represented and bring their own sperm into direct contact with the woman. Other research has indicated that those men who were least comfortable with the idea of having paid for sex were those least likely to want to use a condom with a prostitute. It was too stark a reminder that the encounter was commercially based (Vanwesenbeeck *et al.* 1993).

Finally, although the reported level of condom provision in the area in which we were carrying out our research was high, there nevertheless were occasions in our fieldwork when we were aware of women who were working without access to adequate supplies of condoms:

Penny met us tonight with a relieved 'Am I glad to see you. I had to scrounge some condoms off one of the other lassies the other night.

One woman we approached took condoms saying she had none on her at all. The prostitute drop-in was closed [it was a Sunday] and she was actively touting for business when we met up with her.

Such instances are stark reminders that even with what many of us might regard as near saturation provision of condoms in some areas, nevertheless shortages in availability can still occur which *may* result in the provision of unprotected sex.

Condom failure

In much of this chapter, as well as in much of the literature more broadly, there is a consistent emphasis on condoms and their use in prostitute/client contacts. This is understandable given the lack of other methods of preventing HIV transmission. However it should not be assumed from this focus that condoms are 100 per cent effective in preventing HIV transmission. Although condoms go through rigorous tests to ensure their strength, sensitivity, impermeability etc., we still know very little about their effectiveness and rates of breakage within actual situations of use. A study carried out among female prostitutes in Edinburgh reported that 20 per cent of the women had a condom burst in the previous month (Morgan-Thomas 1990). Our own survey found that 26.4 per cent of the women reported condom failure in the last month (McKeganey and Barnard 1992). De Graaf and colleagues (1993) surveyed 126 female prostitutes and 82 clients in the Netherlands; 49 per cent of the women and 16 per cent of the clients reported having had a condom break during commercial sex. A recent review of what is known about the effectiveness of condoms in reducing HIV transmission suggests that the figure may be either as high as 82 per cent or as low as 46 per cent (Weller 1993). In the light of such a report one would have to conclude that, even with condoms, there remains an element of risk in the transmission of HIV between prostitutes and their clients. Although this may be taken to mean that there is a risk of prostitutes spreading HIV to their clients even in those areas where high levels of condom use have been reported, it is equally the case that such women themselves remain at risk from their clients.

Quantifying the risk of paid sex

The level of risk of HIV transmission between prostitutes and their clients will undoubtedly be very low in those areas where HIV itself is relatively rare among prostitute women. Taking Glasgow as an example, we summarize our HIV data from having tested street prostitutes within that city over two consecutive years in Table 8.

On the basis of these data, one would probably conclude that even if condoms were not being widely used by prostitutes and their clients, the risk of HIV transmission would be fairly low. However, when one combines the low level of HIV with the high level of condom use (even accepting that it may not be as high as claimed), the risks of HIV transmission become very small indeed. The very opposite holds in those countries where HIV infection is high and condom use is low. In Thailand, for example, researchers questioned over 2000 military recruits in 1991. On enrolment into the study 12 per cent of the young men were found to be HIV positive. Fully 81.2 per cent of the men reported past contact with a prostitute. When the men were questioned more closely about the frequency of their prostitute contacts, the researchers found that the risk of the men being HIV positive was highly correlated with the number of occasions on which they had paid for sex. Among those men who reported no

Table 8   HIV infection among Glasgow street prostitutes

	All prostitutes	Prostitutes injecting	Prostitutes not injecting
Year 1			
Number of women tested	159	115	44
Number of women HIV positive	4	4	0
Percentage HIV positive	2.5	3.5	0
Prevalence of HIV 95% (CI)*	0.7%–6.3%	1.0%–8.7%	0.0%–6.6%
Year 2			
Number of women tested	158	127	31
Number of women HIV positive	1	1	0
Percentage HIV positive	0.6	0.8	0
Prevalence of HIV 95% (CI)	0.0%–3.5%	0.0%–4.3%	0.0%–9.2%

* Confidence interval (CI), this is the possible range identified with 95% certainty

prostitute contact, only 2.9 per cent were HIV positive. Among those men who reported weekly prostitute contact, 31.8 per cent were HIV positive (Celentano *et al.* 1993). Such figures are powerful indicators of the additional level of risk involved in commercial sex. None the less it should be stressed again that the figures relate to Thailand – where HIV is widespread among female prostitutes, where many men report contacting prostitutes, and where condom use between prostitutes and clients is inconsistent.

Conclusion

We started this chapter by looking at the results of those studies which have published information on the extent of HIV infection among prostitute women. These studies plainly show the situation as very different depending upon where in the world one looks. While there are striking differences in levels of HIV infection among female prostitutes in the developing and the developed world, it is not the case that HIV is commonplace among prostitutes in all of the developing countries. We reported high rates of infection in some countries in Africa and low rates in others. In terms of the developed countries, overall low levels of infection have been found especially in the case of those women not injecting drugs. Higher levels of infection have been found among those women injecting drugs and those using crack cocaine.

The situation with regard to condom use is also very varied. The broad picture which emerges is one of low levels of condom use in a number of the high HIV prevalence areas and high levels of use in many of the low prevalence areas. On the basis of this information the risks of HIV transmission involving female prostitutes and their clients itself is likely to vary, being high in parts of Africa and Asia and much lower in parts of Europe, North America and Australia.

Prostitutes have been vilified as a reservoir of HIV infection threatening the health of the public in this country as well as in others. Such a response can not only be shown to be incorrect, but also in stark contradiction to the women's efforts at insisting that condoms are used in their sexual contacts with clients. In the UK, as well as elsewhere in Europe and in many parts of North America, Australia and New Zealand, we may well have more grounds to be thankful to female prostitutes for their actions in averting major transmission of HIV than many of us are prepared to admit. Further, whenever unprotected sex takes place between a prostitute and a client (other than where the woman has been raped), the responsibility for that occurrence is held jointly by the prostitute *and* the client. The fact remains that safer sex is the responsibility of both parties. That blame is usually attached to the prostitute is no more than a reflection of our prejudices.

6

Dying for sex: prostitution and violence

If you lose your wits about you in this business you're done for.
(prostitute)

Introduction

To say that prostitution is about sex is to state the obvious; it is also very often about violence (Barnard 1993). Violence was such a frequent occurrence within the street prostitution scene that it was almost commonplace; women expected it to happen at some point and considered themselves lucky if they had so far managed to avoid it. In this chapter we describe the kinds of violence to which the women were routinely subjected, as well as their methods for reducing the likelihood of being attacked. As we will show, the strategies the women adopt to prevent trouble occurring are inherently flawed, both because of the nature of prostitution and the fact that it is an illegal and stigmatized activity. We also consider the link between sex and violence in the context of prostitution and highlight certain parallels between the position of the female prostitute and that of women more generally within our society.

A cautionary note: although violence was reported by nearly all of the women interviewed, only a minority of actual encounters between prostitutes and their clients involved violence. Most encounters proceeded in a straightforward way without any untoward occurrence. Nevertheless the potential for violence was ever present. The women were in agreement that you had to be constantly aware of the possibility of violence and be one step ahead of the client at all times. This view held by the Glasgow street prostitutes can be heard from other prostitutes working on other streets in other cities all over the world (Silbert 1981; Perkins and Bennett 1985; Delacoste and Alexander 1988).

The everyday violence

Prostitution provokes strong reactions from some people; women who work the streets are the most visible representatives of the trade and so also are they the easiest targets for some people's prurient fascinations or loathing or aggression. Streetworking prostitutes have to contend with the whole spectrum of behaviours provoked by the sight of prostitution ranging from name calling to physical assault, rape and murder.

It is a salutary experience to stand on a street alongside a prostitute and observe the reactions of people in the cars cruising by, the faces of solitary drivers, or the groups of young men, and sometimes women, who drive round the red-light area intrigued by the sight of the women:

> As we chatted with Lisa and her friend, a car went by with two men and two women in it. They were very obviously enjoying the spectacle of women prostituting. Lisa said how much it could annoy her. 'I hate it when they do that, especially when it's women. I can sort of understand it when it's men that do it, but not women. I mean, what's big about it?' She added that recently 'a guy wound down his window and shouted out, "Ye clarty [dirty] wee bitch."' This had made her both angry and upset, yet she could do nothing about it.

Such name calling was not infrequently experienced by the women. One might argue that the shouting out of insults could scarcely be classified as violent. However, it is indicative of a pervasive attitude towards women who prostitute, that in so doing they forfeit the right to be treated with respect or even sensitivity and can be the object of people's outrage or anger or derision or be a spectacle for entertainment.

The violence which the women experienced went far beyond name calling and it was perhaps that fact itself which enabled them to be so blasé about the name calling. In a context where there was a real possibility of being raped, beaten and even murdered, there was not a lot of space left to worry about insults hurled from moving cars. The women's fears were well-grounded:

> We met up with Candy whom we had seen earlier that evening shouting the odds at a guy who was walking away from her. She said that she had been in the alley doing business with him when without any warning at all he had punched her hard in the side of her face and made a grab for her bag. She was still holding on to her bag as she recounted this, her lip and cheek bruised and swollen.

> As we were walking along one of the streets this evening we heard a woman screaming nearby; two of the prostitutes were running towards an alley in front of us and we also ran towards the screams. As we turned the corner we saw one of the women whom we had spoken to earlier leaning against the wall nursing her leg. A man in a tracksuit was walking nonchalantly away from her. The woman nursing her leg explained that he had attacked her.

> Jill said that she had just been punched in the face by a man who had asked her to do a double act with the prostitute standing next to her. As she

explained to us what happened the other woman came over to us and confirmed Jill's account.

Marina and I were approached by a woman whom we have chatted to on many nights. She had a black eye and heavily swollen cheekbone. She explained that she had been set upon by a punter earlier that week. He had stopped and asked her for business. Although she had been a bit wary he had used her name. Once in the car she had given him her usual directions to the place she normally used but he had turned on to the motorway. She had protested and he had turned off near the fruit market, pulled the car up near some darkened factories, ordered her to strip and then tied her hands with bin liners. He then punched her in the face and pushed her out of the car. She thought for sure that he had intended running her over but she had managed to scramble over a fence and into a nearby field.

Emma recounted an attack by a client. 'He was a body builder, massive. He was having sex with me for about 20 minutes, that's a long time and nothin' was happening. I asked him to get off me and he got off and I started to get mysel' ready. He pulled the Durex off and started to tuck in his trousers, but then he pulled a gun from the door compartment and said that if I didn't make him come he was gonnae blow ma brains out. I looked at the gun and kept saying to mysel', "That's a gun, that's a gun," and I actually peed mysel'. I knew that if I didn't do exactly what he said he was gonnae shoot me. I thought, "Just play along with him." He raped me, took ages to come and made me do all different things doggie position.'

Such incidents as these represented the backdrop to the women's work. They were recounted by women not in a tone designed to shock or elicit sympathy but with an almost matter-of-fact acceptance − if you worked the streets, sooner or later something similar was going to happen. You could do various things to reduce the likelihood of such incidents occurring but this was unlikely to prevent something happening at some point. As frightening as such violence clearly was, what in a way compounded things was not knowing why some men suddenly took it upon themselves to attack the women. As one woman put it, 'I could understand it if it was for the money, but I mean, we're doing them a service being down here aren't we?'

In Chapter 2 we showed that one of the ways the women attempted to reduce the likelihood of violence was through taking charge of the encounter with the client, issuing clear instructions as to the place, price and manner of the sexual contact. However, the emphasis which women placed on their being in charge could lead them to feel responsible for those occasions where clients had become violent. They appeared to believe that they should have anticipated the potential for such violence and acted accordingly. Such self-chastisement was despite the fact that clients could become violent in an instant without giving any prior indication. Take for example one woman's description of a violent encounter with a client where she blames herself for not having recognized 'the change' in the client's demeanour:

I blame maself really because, as I say, I moved, I'd moved to Fife and went on the drink really bad and I used to drink every time I went up there [red-light area] so in a way I blame it more on maself for not being alert enough. It was weird even now when I think about it – I shouldnae have let it happen. But it was just as if you know one minute he was all right and the next he was . . . what was it . . . 'I'm no' wearin' that condom' you know, the change, you could see it coming. And I'm thinkin' 'OK, just give the guy what he wants and get out of the car . . .'. Ma reactions were that much slower – when I went to open the door he was ten times quicker. By the time I got the door open he was over me and the hands round the throat . . . So I always blame maself mair because I wasnae alert enough . . . He had his hands round ma throat and it's funny, I had on this new shirt and I remember thinkin' 'that's a new shirt', and I was sayin' 'don't, I've got a kid'. After that I flaked out. The next thing was somebody slappin' ma face and I woke up, scratchin' and kickin' and it was the police. Seemingly the car had broken down and he was pushin' it when a security guard had phoned the police. He'd said I was drunk but the police had realized something was wrong. When the CID went to get me out of the car I'd wet masel' and he went 'it's all right hen, no problem'.

Even though the risks of being attacked were so great, the women spent surprisingly little time discussing such incidents. In part the women did not want to keep reminding themselves of what could happen to them because thinking about the risks they ran could be sufficient to stop them working. It was also the case that most women seemed to share the view that you had to come to terms with the reality of that risk yourself – either you faced that risk and carried on working or you stopped working. This was explicitly the rationalization of one woman:

She talked about having recently been raped while working and she'd been afraid to work again but in the end had to come out because she needs the money. She has three daughters to care for, her man's in the jail and she's divorced from the father of her children. She said she'd had to jump from the first floor of a tenement block because the client was so violent. She showed us heavy bruises on her leg and said she'd broken her ankle in the fall, but she'd had to get out. He'd battered her and raped her and she'd thought he might kill her.

This largely individualized response to risk changed dramatically, albeit briefly, when one of the women was found brutally murdered in a nearby park. For a while following the murder, the streets were very quiet. The few women who were working tended to stand in pairs or small groups affording each other a sense of safety though sharing a single topic of conversation:

Earlier that morning we had seen the headline reports of one of the women having been found brutally murdered in a nearby park. The atmosphere on the streets is totally different. There are hardly any women out and those that are seem to be gathered in groups. Every conversation seems to be about Carol [the murdered prostitute]. Nobody seems to know very much about what happened though Helen [prostitute] says she was found in the park, cut open with a bar up her backside. Helen adds that 'a punter's not going to do that, they want sex, they're not going to do that, to

go that far'. This latter seems more designed to reassure Helen herself that
the murderer is not a client and thus that she may not be at risk herself. The
fact remains though that he may well have been a client and that any one
of the cars driving round tonight may be him and any one of the women
may be the next victim. Helen went on to say that she had been with a man
earlier that evening, she thought he had had an Aberdeen accent and there
was a rumour that the murderer might also have an Aberdeen accent since
he had been overheard speaking to the murdered woman. Helen said that
throughout the whole thing with the client her 'fear had been right up'.

In time, despite the fact that the murderer was not caught, the women's
anxieties reduced and the atmosphere in the area returned to a kind of
normality.

Although the women were the victims of most of the violent incidents in the
area, clients too ran the risk of being attacked. There were instances where
clients were attacked by prostitutes' accomplices, usually motivated by the
prospect of financial gain. Finally, and in a way which seemed surprising given
the risks that the women faced from others, there were occasions when
violence would erupt between the women:

Tonight we saw how exploitative the relationships between the women
could be. We were standing in a small group [Enid, Kylie, Julia and us].
Julia left the group and walked over to the opposite corner looking for
business. As she did so, Maureen and another woman rounded the corner
on the same side of the road. As soon as Maureen saw Julia she started
shouting to her and began running over to her. When she caught up with
her she immediately punched her in the face. Enid was watching this
saying to us she was sick of it, that Maureen was stealing Julia's money,
taking £10 off her every night because she knows that Julia earns a fair bit
of money. By this time Maureen had hit Julia on the head with her
handbag and was verbally threatening her. Julia broke away; as she did so
another couple of blows were aimed at her. She came over to where we
were, clearly shaken by what had happened. She said that Maureen had
just put out her cigarette on her breast.

The women's strategies for reducing the risk of violence

Hardly any of the violent incidents that occurred in the area were reported to
the police. Unless the violence itself was of a particularly extreme kind, most of
the women seemed to feel that there was little to be gained from such
reporting. In the first place there appeared to be some doubt that the police
would successfully pursue the men concerned, and a belief that even if they
did, and the case came to court, it would not result in a conviction once it was
known that the woman was working as a prostitute (Scutt 1994). The view
which most women seemed to share was that it was up to them individually,

and to a lesser extent collectively, to find ways of reducing the risks. In this section we look at the various ways of achieving that end.

Taking control of the encounter

As has already been mentioned, the women considered control to be an absolutely essential and integral part of the commercial sex encounter. Through asserting control of the encounter, they sought to create an acquiescent role for the client. In so doing they aimed to reduce the likelihood that the client would try to subvert the terms and conditions of the sex being sold and especially to prevent physical violence. As one woman put it:

> I've got to put it across to them that I'm the one that's in charge and that's it. It's no' as if he's paying me for what he says he wants and he gets what he wants. I say, 'Well, what you want, well that depends if I want to do that, you know what I mean.' You get a lot of them that try to take control, like they'll say 'wait a minute I'm paying this money so I'll say what I want' sort of thing, but as long as you say to them, 'Look you're fuckin' payin' for ma time and you're no' payin' for nothin' else,' that's what I say. 'You pay for the time comin' from the town to ma flat and from the flat to the town and the length of time you're at the flat.' I say things like that when they try to get wide with me.

Not all of the women were as able to be so directive with clients. Women who were new to prostituting, for example, were undoubtedly much less skilled in creating the conditions for client compliance:

> Sheena felt she was a lot more confident with clients now. 'A lot more in control of what I'm doin' whereas before, when I first started, because I was naïve and I didn't really know what was goin' on. I think the guys were in control 'cos they knew, they'd been there before, they knew. They knew that happened whereas I didn't really know so I was just playing along wi' them in a sense. So I mean I got, I was treated like a mug. I mean, every girl that starts down there has nae experience . . .'

Equally, it was difficult to see how women who were heavily under the influence of either alcohol or drugs were in a position to skilfully manage their contact with the client:

> We saw Jean standing at the junction of two roads. As she swayed unsteadily forward and then back it looked as if she might stagger into the road at any moment, oblivious of the oncoming traffic. We went over to her and stood between her and the road. As we did so Jean leant forward towards Marina absently, almost putting her cigarette out on Marina's jacket then reeling back. Looking at Jean in this state it is difficult to see how she could ever take charge of a client. In fact it occurs to me that some clients might even be attracted by her evident lack of control.

Women's intuition

In the absence of any sure-fire way of assessing the advisedness of accepting particular clients the women are obliged to rely on subjective clues. All of the women we spoke to stressed the importance of trusting their intuitive feeling about clients. Clearly it is a part of prostitution that most of the men the women see are complete strangers to them. This means that they have to rely on such things as whether or not they like the 'look' of the client. Different women seemed to emphasize different clues: for one it might be how the man spoke, how he dressed, his general demeanour, whether he had glasses on, for another it would be the general state of his car etc. The women placed especial importance on assessing the mannerisms and behaviour of clients. Whether or not the client engaged with the woman was regarded by most as an important clue; a man who refused to talk or look at the woman would be interpreted as signalling danger:

> 'The main thing is if they don't talk to me, see if they don't talk to me, you know you got trouble, you know. . . .' She instanced having got into a car with a client. 'Say I say, "my name's Lynette, pleased to meet you," and they'll say, "my name's Bob," and that's it, and then you'll say be driving along, ten minutes, you know it's like drawing teeth. If they don't speak to me, it's as if they're tryin' to hide somethin' if they don't talk to you and that freaks me out, 'cos then I can't suss them out. If they'll not talk to me then I cannae suss them out.'

Despite the importance placed upon intuition, there were still occasions where women had agreed to provide certain men with sexual services against their better judgement and had then found it interactionally difficult to refuse the same client the next time around:

> Neil and I were stood talking to Ellie when a car went by driven by a man waiting for Ellie to give him the nod and go with him for business. She turned her back on him and said to us and Jane, who'd just come over, 'He's always stoppin' for me, he's done it every time he's gone by, but I'll no' go wi' him. I don't know he jus' gies me the creeps.' Jane responded, 'Aye, he keeps on stoppin' for me an' all, but I don't like him either, I'll no' go wi' him.' Ellie said that she had in fact done business with him twice before but somehow he really frightened her. 'It's difficult when you've done business wi' them before, can't really make excuses. I mean I do say things like "no, I'm cut" or "I'm bleeding" or "I can only do oral" [this client only likes sex], but you cannae really keep on makin' excuses.'

Working rules

Apart from such intuitive judgements, women also maintained certain self-imposed rules which were designed to lessen the threats to their safety. Such measures included avoiding certain 'types' of clients, not working beyond certain times of night or never going with more than one client at a time.

'I don't do walkers – dodgy.' She then went on to explain that she had recently seen the film *Silence of the Lambs* and how it had really frightened her. 'I just have to keep reminding myself that doesnae happen in Glasgow. See if I think about it I get really paranoid. If I saw you walking about [she directed this comment at Neil] I wouldnae do business with you.' Neil asked why. She replied, 'Well as I say I don't do walkers and anyway you look dodgy.'

One woman we spoke to said that she didn't like to work beyond midnight: 'That's when you get the dodgy ones.'

As Neil gave condoms to Elaine a car drew up with three men in it. Elaine dismissed them until she realized she knew one of them, he's a regular of hers. He'd come to look for business with her and was wanting her to provide it to all three of them – she refused to go and walked back. Then Fiona [another prostitute] suggested they do a 'doubler' and go together so then Elaine wouldn't feel so outnumbered. The men didn't agree to this, they wanted Elaine on her own. Elaine said the only way she'd do it would be one at a time. She'd go with one man in the car to the flat and when he was finished he'd come back to the town to pick up the next man. As she explained this to them the man she knew got out of the motor, joking about being left to walk. She laughed but turned back to the two men still in the car saying 'c'mon, I said one in the motor, no' two, I'll go back wi' one'.

Such 'rules' would cover not only the number of clients a woman was prepared to go with but also which seat in a client's car she would occupy:

First person we saw tonight was Katy getting out of a car. She came over to us asking for needles. She mentioned a woman who had been working the same spot as her and asked if we had seen her. Apparently she had not yet returned and Katy was beginning to be concerned. 'She went wi' two Pakis away in a motor.' Thinking that this was what was concerning Katy, we asked if she went with two men in the car; Katy dismissed this saying that she had done business with two men the previous night. What bothered Katy was the fact that she had sat in one of the back seats of the client's car. 'You should never do that. See me I say, "I'm no' bein' cheeky but I wantae sit in the front," that way if anything happens I can kick the windae out.' She added that she would have to speak to the woman on her return.

Working with other women

Although women generally worked on their own it was not uncommon for two or more women to agree to keep an eye out for each other. This could take the form of noting down the registration number of a car as it drove off, or a woman watching at the end of an alley where sex was being provided. In the event of a client threatening violence, the claim that a friend had noted down the registration, thereby making him easily traceable by the police, might be an effective counter ploy. Similarly, being able to call to another woman nearby might mean an attacker would run away before inflicting serious injury on the woman.

Another strategy which some women employed was to work with a boyfriend or husband nearby. The presence of such men, while increasing the safety of certain women, could also increase the risks faced by clients:

> Janice had been working at 4 a.m. As it was so late her pal Colin had been there with her. She'd gone down an alley to give a guy oral sex for £10; Colin had stood at the end of the lane to look out for her. The client had told her he'd recently been ripped off by another prostitute and so didn't want to pay until afterwards. 'I agreed to it, first time I ever done it, stupid of me it was. At the end he goes "I've nae money, I've only got £3" so I called Colin over. He said, "gonnae let me see your wallet." He said he didn't have a wallet so Colin just laid into him. We got his wallet off him, £95 it had in it. I wouldnae have taken it but that he started holdin' me up. If he'd come out wi' the tenner he'd have saved all the bother.'

Despite being favoured by some women the police actively discouraged the presence of such men believing that they inevitably lead to an increase in the tension within the red-light area.

Carrying weapons

Carrying an offensive weapon is a criminal offence within the United Kingdom for which an individual can be arrested, fined and in some cases jailed. Having said this, very many of the women had access to a weapon while working. These could be combs with sharpened handles, needles, knives, irritant sprays imported from other countries etc. Women who took clients back to their flats would sometimes make sure that they were within easy reach of such weapons:

> I've got a big hammer that I keep by the side of ma bed so if any punter starts tryin' anythin' on he'll get what's what.

Effectiveness

None of these strategies ensured the women's safety. Indeed, it is arguable that the very nature of what the women were doing, entering cars or dark alleys with complete strangers, can never be anything other than extremely dangerous. These strategies were the only means within the women's own grasp to try and reduce their chances of being attacked. It is impossible to know how effective any of the above strategies were in avoiding actual instances of violence. Nevertheless they provided the women with a degree of confidence enabling them to work in the face of their own knowledge that they were dealing with men whose behaviour was, for the most part, completely unpredictable. In this sense the women were like gamblers, only the risk was not of winning, but losing, and they each had their own systems for lessening the chances of that outcome.

In the remainder of this chapter we look at the links between violence and sex and in particular at the relationship between notions of the 'proper' behaviour of women and the prostitute who represents the social opposite of that role.

Explaining sexual violence

Sexual violence, it has been pointed out before, is not about sex but about power. At the heart of such violence is the structurally subordinate position of women in society. Within our society, and many others, power, authority and control are attributes normatively invested in men and not women. Quite apart from the ways in which the expectation of male dominance impacts on the workings of society, it is clear that it definitively shapes the structural relations between men and women. Part of the process of male role socialization incorporates the notion that women are subordinate to men, that they should be under the control of men, and that they should be protected by them, as well as being punished and disciplined by them when deemed necessary (Dobash and Dobash 1979; Sanday 1986; Scully 1990).

In a pioneering study of convicted male rapists, Scully (1990) noted the way in which the men's justifications for rape were rooted in ideas as to how a woman ought properly to act. Their perception of certain women as violating those expectations was offered by them as sufficient reason for having raped them. Plainly, the motivations of convicted rapists cannot be taken as representing those of men more broadly. None the less, setting aside the extremity of these men's actions, the views that informed them are structurally rooted in notions of 'proper' female behaviour. In the minds of these men there was justification for rape if a woman had dressed provocatively, had been too forward in her manner, or had used drugs or alcohol. In fact, the men Scully interviewed would characterize *any* behaviour which contradicted stereotypes of appropriate female behaviour as being a major reason for the woman being raped. As far as the rapists were concerned such behaviour meant that the woman had waived her rights to be treated with respect and was inviting abuse. Scully's study provides evidence that some men at least used rape as a way of asserting their dominance over women. Similarly in interviews with a wide range of men, Chesler (1978) found that the desire to dominate women was an enduring male fantasy.

The importance of male expectations as to how women ought to act is further underlined by the narrowness of those expectations. A good woman is ideally a wife and mother whose sexuality is expressed within the context of a loving family relationship (Dobash and Dobash 1979; Horowitz 1981). From a very early age, girls are made aware of the link between social respectability and sexual purity (James 1986; Holland *et al.* 1992). A woman who is seen as sexually available risks losing her reputation. The dichotomy of women as either madonna or whore (Stanko 1985) whereby the madonna resists sexual advances but the whore invites them, leads to the assertion that nice girls don't get raped, or, if they do, it is somehow a more monstrous assault than the rape of a prostitute. It is interesting to note in this respect that there was a qualitative shift in both the media coverage and the police investigation of the hunt for the British serial killer known as the Yorkshire Ripper once it was revealed that the latest victim had not been a prostitute but an 'innocent' female student (Smith 1993).

The occurrence of violence within the prostitute/client encounter can be understood as part of the way in which women in this society, at least, are defined apropos of men (Miller and Schwartz 1995). The prostitute violates fundamental expectations as to how women ought to act. In the first place she is overtly selling sex, dressing for sex, making herself available for sex. As Pheterson points out, 'prostitutes serve as models of female unchastity. As sexual solicitors they are assumed to invite violence' (1988: 225). A woman who prostitutes already violates norms of how women ought to act and calls forth her own violation. It is this model of thinking which asserts that prostitutes cannot be raped because of the work they do (Pheterson 1990). That these attitudes are widespread in society is evidenced by the fact that hardly any of the violence to which prostitutes are subjected is reported to the police. Rightly or wrongly, such women anticipate the reaction that they are in effect the perpetrators of their own violent assault, by placing themselves in the situation where such assaults are a likely occurrence (Silbert 1981; Delacoste and Alexander 1988; Frohmann 1991).

Such attitudes are also instilled in the legal systems of some countries. In 1991 Judge Jones of the Victorian County Court in Australia explained his award of a relatively lenient sentence to a man who had raped a prostitute by saying that as a result of her work the woman would have been less psychologically damaged than a chaste woman. Despite the public outcry which followed this sentence, and an appeal to the Supreme Court of Victoria, the decision was allowed to stand (Scutt 1994).

Women who prostitute can be seen as violating male expectations of appropriate female behaviours not only with respect to publicly soliciting sex but also in taking an overt stance in managing the sexual encounter. Among many men, including some of the clients we interviewed, there was a clear expectation that they should be in charge of the sexual encounter – the fact that they had the money to pay for the sex simply underlined their power. It is worth noting in this respect that at least one of the strategies which the women employed to reduce their risk of violence – taking control of the encounter – may paradoxically have increased those risks so far as certain men were concerned.

So long as prostitutes are seen as no more than the sex they sell, the violence which we have described in this chapter will continue. For this to alter there needs to be a fundamental change in how we see prostitution. We have to understand the motivations and experiences of those who sell sex and those who buy sex. Similarly there is a need to challenge the perception of prostitutes as easy victims – as victims who can be attacked at little or no personal cost. Most of the clients who are violent towards prostitute women know that the likelihood of the woman reporting such an attack is slight. Moreover, even if such an attack is reported, the client has the protection of his public *same rights.*

respectability whereas the prostitute is seen as having sacrificed hers in her work (Scutt 1992). Society's expectations in this respect serve to bind the woman to the violence of her work. The need is to change those expectations and to ensure that where such violence is reported it is treated with the same seriousness as violence directed at any other member of society.

In the next chapter we shift our focus from the public arena of the red-light area to consider the impact of the women's work on their personal lives.

7

Women as prostitutes, women as lovers: the management of identity

Introduction

When a woman agrees to sell sex to a man she agrees to the provision of a service. She might provide him with vaginal sex, or oral sex, she might dress up for him, she might agree to dress him up. Paramount in the woman's dealings with the client is the fact that this is a commercial transaction. However, the sale of the body for purposes of sex differs from most business transactions in the sense that it has direct inroads into the realms of private sexual experience. The same body which is used for commercial purposes can also be a vehicle for the expression of such things as emotional commitment, pleasure and desire. In this chapter we consider the social management of a stigmatized identity (that of prostitute), both in terms of everyday life and particularly in the context of private, meaningful relationships outside of prostitution. We will show how the women worked to maintain a distinction between these domains of experience in their working practices and in their private lives.

It is worthwhile to begin by asking the question why it is that prostitutes seek to separate commercial from private sex. So too is it important to look at the range of strategies that women use to enforce that distinction. As might be imagined the degree to which these distinctions are hard and fast is something of an open question. The trading of sex for money can have direct repercussions for the private lives of women, particularly in their private sexual relationships with others.

The public body and the inner self

The distinction between use of the body for commercial purposes and for private sexual expression presents a highly fragile mental construct – after all, it is physically the same body, and how different can acts like vaginal or oral sex be? None the less, the women in this study, as in other studies (McLeod 1982; Day 1990) reported that they made an absolute distinction between private and commercial sex. Individual prostitutes might vary in the mechanisms they used to enforce the distinction but they were united in retaining a sense of the necessity of that difference. The reasons why this distinction was considered important appeared to centre around the protection of their personal identities and lives from being devalued by their work as prostitutes. The degree to which the women were actually successful in retaining an absolute distinction should perhaps be seen more as an ideal than a reality.

None of the women with whom we were in contact openly embraced the identity of prostitute; rather it was worn as a mantle to be shrugged off at the point at which work ceased. The women were actively engaged in a process of managing conflicting identities, one of which they perceived themselves as having adopted temporarily and out of expediency. Their other identity was the one which appeared to be viewed as their essential 'real' self. The management of these identities was through separation. For the purposes of commercial sex the body was objectified – in a very real sense it was emptied of meaning. That this separation is important can be evidenced by the effort and care women put into the creation of strategies which would distance their role as prostitutes from their everyday lives.

Before looking at the various strategies the women used to try to contain their involvement in prostitution, it is worth briefly considering the notion of spoiled identity and its management in everyday life. For all its long history, prostitution remains a stigmatized activity; selling sex is no more socially acceptable now than in the past. Women who engage in prostitution are of course aware of this; it is this awareness of what is deemed to be their failing, their social defilement, that opens the possibility of shame. As Goffman notes in his essay on the nature of social stigma, it is because the stigmatized individual 'acquires identity standards which he applies to himself in spite of his failing to conform to them that he will feel some ambivalence about his own self' (1963: 130). It is this ambivalence which leads many women to try to manage their identity by separating off the defiling influence of prostitution and defining it as largely an irrelevance in so far as personal (as opposed to social) identity is concerned. To achieve this requires not only the maintenance of certain rituals to mark the separation, some of which we will discuss later, but also a commitment to managing the flow to others of information about their involvement in prostitution. This may take the form of concealing the fact of working as a prostitute, or just eliding the details of the work. If as social beings we are in large part concerned about how we are viewed in the eyes of others it is no surprise that controlling information should be an important means of managing personal identity.

Little attention appears to have been paid to the ways in which the women might seek to keep their work as prostitutes discrete from their other social and personal roles. Where the issue has been considered, it has generally focused almost exclusively on the use of condoms. With all the attention that has been paid to the use of condoms as a barrier to HIV and other sexually transmitted infections, it has become something of a convention to point also to their additional use as a symbolic barrier between client and the prostitute. It is certainly true that many prostitutes will describe the condom as providing this function; it is also the case that this is not the only means that prostitutes employ to make good the distinction. The mental separation between mind and body which prostitutes aim to achieve during the provision of commercial sex is the key issue. The condom should be seen as an additional, overt, means of facilitating that distance. If one stops to consider the enormity of what the women want to achieve in trying to retain an absolute distinction between these realms of experience it becomes difficult to believe that the placing of a thin rubber sheath could, in and of itself, so conclusively resolve potential conflicts of identity or ambiguity between roles. In the next section we will consider those other strategies employed by the women to establish a distance between their work and their other lives.

Although only one woman, Sheena, referred specifically to having a 'switch' which prevented her from engaging with the client in any other way than the purely physical, it was apparent that many others engaged in a similar process:

> Sheena said that many of her clients wanted to know what the difference was between having sex with them and with her boyfriends. 'I say, "Well, the best way to explain is like a wee switch I've got in ma head that I can completely switch off."'

Rituals of separation

An important means whereby many women created distance was to have very specific rituals marking off their everyday roles from their roles as prostitutes. Women would describe, often in great detail, the preparations they made for going out to work and what they did on their return. So for example they would talk about putting on their make-up, dressing (in clothes that were only used for the purpose of prostitution) and often also taking a drink or drugs in readiness for their stepping out as a prostitute. The deliberate and methodical way in which many of the women described their preparations suggested their importance as markers of separation:

> Every night, every night I have a bath before I go out, when I'm sitting here putting ma make-up on, you psyche yourself up, you cannae really explain what I say to myself or what I actually do. You just, you know you're goin' out to work and you just och, build yoursel' up for it. You don't jus' sit and think well I'm gointae be doin' this or I'm gointae be doin' that, but it is, I mean it's the same routine every night. I'm goin' out to work what I do, so in a way it is psyching yoursel' up.

In essence many of these activities of washing, selecting the right clothes etc. were similar to those adopted by workers in a wide range of jobs. In the case of prostitution, however, they held a special significance in serving to limit the impact of the women's work on their sense of self and family life – they served to bracket off the women's work from their wider lives:

> I get ma shower, do the hair, do the face and get ma workin' clothes out.

It is striking how this woman refers to 'the hair' and 'the face' as objects physically separate from herself – her hair and her face become not an expression of her individuality and personality but a tool in the process of her work. Getting ready for work entails the detailed preparation of both mind and body:

> I keep ma clothes in the wardrobe, they're for ma work and I never wear them apart from that. Anyway I sit there on the sofa and basically I switch off. I have ma cup of tea before I go. I say, 'Right that's it that's me.' I go and phone for ma taxi. I've seen me drag ma feet sometimes, more now the way it is up there. You look at the clock. 'I need to go. . . .' Ma daughter will tell you, it gets to the stage that if I didnae have to, I wouldnae.

The routines of the drug-injecting prostitutes differed only in that their preparation for work invariably involved their having a 'hit' before working:

> About 6 o'clock I get ready. I put on ma make-up and fix ma hair, then I have a hit [inject drugs], put on ma clothes and go for ma taxi. If I haven't had a hit you just want it over and done with and if you've had a hit you can stand it.

The return from work involved a parallel process, in this case not of the construction of the work persona but of its dismantlement, a process which entailed coming to terms with what the evening's work may have entailed:

> I go for ma bath that's what I do, get in ma bath and relax, just become me, it's like two different people.

> When I finish work and I'm back here [home] the first thing I do is get the clothes off. I'll come in maybe stick the kettle on and everything comes off, it's put into the washing machine and I get ma shower.

These rituals of separation, of changing their clothes, having baths and showers, having a hit of drugs or taking a drink or sitting quietly is little different to the kinds of things many people do when they get home from work and want to relax. However the women's descriptions of this time gave a definite impression of a sloughing off of an assumed identity.

Managing distance from clients

Once the woman was in the red-light area and at work, the most commonly reported strategy was one of objectifying the body by refusing the possibility of stimulation and pleasure. The following field extract is illustrative in this regard as the woman in relating the conversation she had with another prostitute is describing her refusal to be physically aroused by a client and moreover her repugnance at the thought of it. She is also pointing to the means by which she refuses the possibility of pleasure through concentrating on the money and the fact that this is a financial transaction, nothing more. Although the woman is reporting a conversation, her incredulity that any woman could enjoy sexual contact with a client is noteworthy, as indeed is the purported fact that the woman being discussed found it difficult to avoid becoming sexually aroused by clients:

> . . . she says to me, 'Do you ever enjoy it when ye go wi' a punter?' I says, 'No,' she says, 'No!' And I went, 'I hate them,' and she went, 'Oh I do.' I says, 'How do you?' an' she says, 'Like do you ever come [orgasm] when you're wi' a punter?' 'cos she does all the time. She says, 'How do you turn yerself off?' I says, 'Quite fuckin' easy, look the other way and think o' the money ye know what I mean.'

The woman speaking below similarly articulated her refusal to be aroused specifically in terms of the fact that she was prostituting and that enjoyment of sex would in some sense degrade her as a person. So even though clients might be sexually skilled it remains important to her integrity not to allow contacts between herself and clients to be anything other than strictly functional:

> I asked Maria if she ever enjoyed sex with punters. Her immediate reply was, 'I don't let myself. I mean some of them I suppose you know, they know how to touch right, the difficult thing is when some of them want to give you oral sex. But I mean, I'm one of those lucky people, I can cut off. I just like think of something else. I never let myself enjoy it, just because it's fun for me. Some of the girls do and Mike [her lover] says to me, "Why not, you know, why not let yourself enjoy it and just make it fun." But it's bad enough, you feel bad enough about yourself, you know you're up there for money and that's it, let alone thinking you're up there for fun. I don't ever let mysel' enjoy it.'

Although it is difficult to be categorical given the obvious complexity of these women's feelings about prostitution in terms of self-worth, none the less it is apparent that neither woman considered it appropriate to enjoy their commercial sex contacts. In the course of our fieldwork we only ever met one woman who claimed that it was possible to enjoy sex with a client, depending on how good-looking and how sexually skilled he was. For the rest, though, there was no apparent inclination to experience sex with a client as anything other than as a means to an end. Focusing on the money that the client represented was a means of de-personalizing the client and of refusing to see him in any other light than as someone whom requested sexual acts were performed on.

This finding, while generally borne out in other studies (see, for example, Day 1990; Pheterson 1990) is contrary to that reported by Savitz and Rosen (1988). These researchers found prostitutes did derive sexual pleasure from their commercial sexual contacts. Their sexual enjoyment was much greater with their private partners; nevertheless, they experienced sexual pleasure with their clients. This is sharply at odds with the way in which Glasgow street prostitutes tended to describe their commercial sex contacts:

> 'The honest truth is, when I'm there I'm jus' thinking, "Well that's £10 for this and £10 for that," like that. That's what I'm thinkin' about.' Apparently a client had the other week said to her, 'You're a bit cool aren't you?' To this

Trudy replied, 'Listen hen, you're wi' a prostitute, you want to make love, you go with someone else.'

The degree to which the women de-personalized their contacts with clients can perhaps be illustrated through anecdote. Part of our contact with the women included use of a short questionnaire asking them about different facets of their work. One question asked how many clients they had had sexual contact with on the last night worked. The way in which the women worked this out was *not* to add up individual clients, but to consider the amount of money they had made in total and, working back from this, consider the money made from each client in terms of the sex act performed. The individual client had no apparent significance, it was only the sex act and the money made from it which appeared to matter.

It might be thought that the situation with regard to regular clients would be different. However, in essence they did not appear to be seen much differently. Some prostitutes have been providing the same men with sexual services for years and have developed cordial, even friendly relations with them. However, regular or not, these men share in common the fact that they purchase sex and this marks them off from other men in a fundamental sense (Lewis 1985). This separation is evident from the comments below where a woman was asked to describe the difference between clients and contacts with men in her private life. Her simple response was:

'I fancy them. . . .' She then went on to talk about men who bought sex from her. 'There are some good-looking guys, I mean some honeys, ye know, and they go away an' you think, "Oh, oh why I never met him up at the dancin'."'

The woman recognizes their attractiveness but laments the fact that she did not meet any of them in another context where it would be possible for her to feel attracted to them. In the context of prostitution, however, attractiveness is largely an irrelevance. Many other prostitutes similarly discounted seeing a client in any other light than as a man to whom they sold sexual services regardless of any attractive physical or personal attributes they might possess. One woman explained:

I've got a rule that I never get involved with punters . . . it's too difficult, I mean, if they've paid you for sex and then you're, you know . . . it's too complicated. I wouldn't get involved with punters anyway but I mean I'm not saying all punters are bad, but, I mean, people got needs and all the rest of it but . . . nah . . . it's not my scene, some girls do it but I don't.

Interestingly, this woman did say that she had at one point become involved with a client. It may be that it was this experience which particularly informed her view that having a relationship with a man to whom you had previously sold sex raised too many complications.

We did contact one other woman who had become the sexual partner of a former client. The potential for conflict may perhaps be evidenced in her description of his behaviour towards her:

Kit is one of the older prostitutes and doesn't really make very much money partly because of her age. She is also a bit simple. She talked about her man whom she said she'd met through prostitution. When we last met her she was wondering if the bruising on her legs came from her man pushing her down the stairs or she'd fallen. She was drunk at the time. She described being in the pub with him and his friends. 'He goes to his friends about me, "Imagine payin' a fiver to fill that hole; I must have been mad" and I goes, "Aye, and you're gettin' it free the now!"'

For the most part prostitutes seem to regard clients in as impersonal a way as possible. They are selling a sexual service, end of story. Some women had a sense of professionalism such that they would try to ensure that the man was able to relax, that he got sexual satisfaction, but this was as far as it went. Comments which women made about commercial sex like 'a willy is a wallet' or that it was 'like doin' the housework' emphasized their essential detachment from clients in terms other than the purely professional:

> I'm a business woman. I try an' do ma best. They're payin' me for it and this is ma business. This is how I earn ma livin'. I don't jus' take the money and go 'och, fuck 'em'. They're gettin' what they paid for, that's the way I work. But only what they pay for and no more. So I do ma best.

Prostitutes reported having male clients who for one reason or another wanted them to be sexually aroused. Perhaps some men wanted to mask the true nature of the interaction – that they are paying to make use of a woman's body. Perhaps some wanted to affirm their sense of male prowess by, as one woman described it, 'doing something to a prostitute no man's ever done before'. The women's reactions to client efforts to sexually arouse them were a mixture of indifference, tolerance and sometimes derision:

> She says she plays it straight with punters and won't pretend to be excited. Some punters try to get her worked up saying, 'I'm gonnae get you goin' first,' to which she replies, 'well ye'll be here all night if you do that.'

> Anita remarked how men were desperate for you to enjoy sex with them. 'You're lying there making all the right noises and that, but at the same time you're lookin' out the car windae and calculating what it'll buy you, you know, "oh good that's the weans' shoes out of the way", that kind of thing.'

Prostitutes are not unique in making a distinction between physical presentations of self and their own privately held beliefs (or what might be termed the 'inner self'). Hochschild (1983), in a study of US airline flight attendants, demonstrates how they were trained not just in the mechanics of providing a service, but also to display an emotional commitment to the welfare and comfort of airline passengers. Flight attendants are trained to show a caring, courteous, friendly and efficient front, even in the face of rude, arrogant or sexist passengers. Hochschild describes this as the commercialization of feeling. Clearly it is not directly analogous to the experience of prostitution since streetworking women are generally working informally for themselves and so are not obliged in the same way to manufacture a response to the client. However, in a similar fashion to the flight attendants whose courteousness and efficiency is in part directed towards encouraging repeat custom, so too do many prostitutes cast an eye to generating future business by adopting an equivalent professionalism. What prostitutes and flight attendants do share in common is a separation of realms of experience into private and public domains. Flight attendants' faces and feelings come to take on the property of a resource to make money, although not directly for themselves. Prostitutes' bodies are similarly a resource to make money. In both cases 'the body, not the soul, is the main tool of the trade' (Hochschild 1983: 37).

The problem for women who prostitute is perhaps more acute because sex is generally a vehicle for the expression of such things as desire, love, affection and commitment for another human being. A smile and a display of caring does not have such direct inroads into private expressions of meaning. This may mean that prostitutes have even more invested in maintaining that distinction as a means of holding onto their own self-esteem and of not devaluing their private sexual relationships.

The most visible strategy prostitutes use to distance themselves from clients is explicitness. From the outset they make clear that they are sexually available but only at a price. This explicitness enables the prostitute firstly to assert her intention to be in control of her dealings with clients. It also removes at a swipe any misapprehension as to the commercial nature of sexual contact between prostitute and client. A very clear example of this explicitness was demonstrated in an earlier quoted fieldnote extract when a client initially walked by a prostitute. He then turned abruptly and went back to her. Holding an unlit cigarette he asked her if she had a light for it. Without batting an eyelid she responded, 'Aye, and I don't do it outside by the way.' She had correctly surmised that the man was sexually interested in her but immediately pre-empted any ambiguity over the true nature of the contact he had initiated. Similarly when men invite prostitutes out to dinner or for a drink the women generally make explicit that the interaction whether social or sexual is commercially based. Clearly much of the reason for this is financial. However it also serves to underline the fact that the reason for their liaison is purely commercial, whatever the client may feel about it:

> I mean some of my punters are all right and that, regularly phone up just to talk to me or maybe come up even if they're no' wantin' business. . . . I mean a few of them are OK they invite me out to dinner and want to take me out and things, but I charge them for that.

As prostitutes themselves say, the majority of men are not interested in setting up a personal relationship. Mostly they want a sexual service without complications. There are however men who try to blur the distinction between the woman selling sex and the woman 'inside'. Particularly problematic are those clients who fall in love with prostitutes:

> Oh I hate that, really that is ma hate, when they try and get all lovey dovey. I mean t'me any guy that tries to get lovey dovey with a prostitute is off his head. . . . You always get the one that's 'I really like you and why are you doing this . . .' and I just hate that. I mean I've had one guy in a big fight. . . . I stopped having him because it was just a nightmare, he was going 'I love you, I love making love to you. . . .'. I used to say, 'If that is

what you call making love you are one wimp' [laughs]! I mean I had to speak to this guy because he was in love with a prostitute and you don't fall in love with prostitutes, and this guy was, I mean, I broke this guy's heart.

Prostitutes were often frankly amazed by clients who confused bought sex with expressive, emotional sex. Many indeed doubted the sanity of such men and would preface stories by indicating that they thought them simple or just crazy. One woman felt they confused her work image (laughing, chatting, sexy, sociable) with her real person:

> They don't realize that during the day you're in your jeans, big sweatshirt on, doing shopping, washing and cleaning, looking after your weans. They think you wake up like a film star with nothing to do and make-up perfect, with your legs wide open for them.

This woman felt that such men were subscribing to the image of the prostitute as permanently sexually receptive and as probably working not so much to make money as for the opportunity to have sex with numerous men.

As well as maintaining an explicit stance as to the nature of the sexual encounter, prostitutes make decisions as to the kinds of sexual services they will supply to clients. Much of the motivation for this appears to come from a desire to retain some sex acts as exclusive to their private relationships, as was the case for the woman quoted below:

> We were talking about how Annette made the distinction between sex with her clients and with her partner. ''Cos I don't feel nothin' when I'm out there, I don't feel a thing and because of the things that I don't do out there like kiss and oral sex. I mean anal sex I don't do that at all wi' anybody [laughs] but they two things I enjoy and I keep them for mysel'. I mean I do enjoy sex wi' Todd because it's different, I mean, I'm involved in it, I'm responding.'

It has been widely reported that prostitutes do not kiss clients (Shedlin 1990; Perkins and Bennett 1985). However there do not appear to be any hard and fast rules over what is and what is not permissible. Rather individual women make decisions about what they are prepared to provide. On balance the majority of women do not like to kiss clients. One woman remarked upon their bad breath, rotten teeth and the sheer unpleasantness of a client coming at you with his tongue out. Other women described a similar aversion but less in physical terms than as an intrusion into their private lives. One woman explained that she would not kiss punters because it was 'crossing the line', it was too private an act. The thought of kissing a punter was physically repugnant to her. Other women however did not have the same attitude towards kissing as exclusive to their private relationships. As one woman said:

> There's two guys that kiss but they pay for it . . . I don't like them doing it but they're wantin' it and you're no' doin' anything else wi' them. They're just playin' wi' themselves while you're kissin' them, so it's no' so bad. They're regulars.

It is notable that while she would allow kissing with two clients, there were other acts which she would not contemplate. She did not allow anal sex (very few women appeared to) or men to provide her with oral sex. With regard to the latter she simply commented that she preferred to touch them and not have them touching her. Possibly she felt that this was too personal an act, or that she wanted to retain this as something shared between herself and her partner. Possibly also this increased the likelihood that she might be sexually aroused which would collapse the distance between her role as prostitute and her personal identity.

As we saw in Chapter 2, often women would make a decision to provide either only oral sex or only vaginal sex. This may seem surprising given the stereotypical picture of the prostitute as there purely to fulfil male desires for a price. Women would often refuse clients on the basis that they were not prepared to provide certain sexual services. Partly this would relate to the unpleasantness of certain acts, partly also to notions of personal pride. This latter was demonstrated by a woman who refused a client who bid her take her clothes off and provide oral sex in an alley:

> I'm no' gonnae be on ma knees for a tenner, I've got ma pride.

Clearly women who would only provide one or other of the two most requested sexual services were limiting their potential to earn money. However it was apparent that some women were prepared to forgo this if it meant not having to provide a type of sex service.

Beyond such distancing strategies as refusing to provide clients with certain sexual services and retaining an essential emotional detachment, some women reported a need to use drugs or alcohol specifically to numb their awareness of the work they were doing:

> If I've no' had a hit, you jus' want it over an' done with. If you've had a hit, you can stand and work nae bother, it doesnae bother you, you know what I mean. But ye see if you're straight, ye start to think about it, then things start flooding back intae your mind and you're sayin' 'I don't want to dae this', you know what I mean.

To an extent this may be something of a post hoc rationalization since many of the drug-using women at least were prostituting to fund an already established drug habit. None the less drug-using prostitutes would all report injecting drugs before beginning the night's work and a good many cited that part of the reason for this was to give them Dutch courage. This is certainly uppermost in this woman's mind:

> Gabby [a drug injector] greeted us with indignation that she had been arrested by the police for soliciting when in fact she had not been. She said she'd been in the jail from 2.30 to 10.00 p.m. so she was withdrawing. She needed 50p. 'Ten bob that's all I need so as I can get a can [of beer] to get my bottle [courage] thegether so I can work. I need to get my bottle and then I can do it, sounds silly doesn't it, but that's what I need.'

Even with drugs or alcohol many women knew they could not blank out the reality of the work they did as prostitutes and the shame that some felt for doing it:

It doesnae matter how much you take or what you take, you've still got to wake up in the morning and go 'I done that, I went out and I done that'. Nothing's going to stop you waking up next day and knowing what you done last night.

A lot o' them think it's right easy, y'know. Like some of them'll say, 'Youse'll get easy money.' But I say, 'How can ye think it's easy because of what I'm doin' wi' you? You know what I mean? But I don't think it's easy because I've got to go wi' ye and I've got to think about it after it.' They don't think about it, they jus' go home to their wives as if nothin's happened.

From the accounts provided by prostitutes it was apparent that they were concerned to mark the distinction between commercial and private sex. It was also clear that there was no one way to distinguish these experiences. Condoms are clearly not the only or even the most important means by which prostitutes separate clients from lovers or partners. The important point is to make the distinction; the means of doing so is significant given that women employ a multiplicity of means for marking off commercial from private, personal sexual experience.

Conflicting roles

In the preceding section the focus largely centred on the ways in which prostitutes seek to establish the boundaries of their involvement with clients, their chief concern being to retain a certain emotional detachment from the sale of the body to clients. The following section will more closely concern itself with the degree to which these strategies successfully operate to protect prostitute women's private lives and their relationships.

Once work had finished for the evening, many women made a conscious decision to 'forget' or switch off from the preceding hours. Some would do this by concentrating on the money they had earned and what it would buy them. This was especially apparent among drug-using prostitutes whose financial needs were often more immediately acute:

Ye forget all about it when you come home. You've just got the money an' that's all ye care about then.

For some women this transformation was much harder to effect. They reported finding it difficult to switch off from thinking about what had happened in the last few hours. There did appear to be a learning curve though, as women reported finding it easier over time to control the passage of their thoughts:

I asked Lynette what she did when she got home at night, whether or not she ever felt emotional about it or would she just shut off from it. She responded, 'Well, now I don't, I used to get very emotional about it. Think about it, that's the worst thing you can do. Come home and sit down and think, you wouldn't cry or anything but it would knock you off your head. I mean if you sat down every night and thought about what you had done.'

However, for at least one woman, and quite possibly others, the sale of sex never became any easier over time to compartmentalize and so neutralize. Her stated inability to switch off from working as a prostitute quite substantially undermined her relationship with her partner:

Now I get into the town about 7 o'clock. I'm coming in at 10 and I'm knackered and I jus' wantae sleep so I'm lying there and I don't talk or anythin' y'know what I mean 'cos I start tae think about what I've done jus' before I've come in and then I'll sit there and then I'll go [makes the sound of retching]. It turns your stomach. Then I go to ma bed and the two of us'll lie in our bed and I'll get up and come in here [front room] and sit. I cannae get it out o' ma head that it's him, and no' another punter. Y'know what I mean? So I end up gettin' up and comin' in here and jus' sittin'.

In the mind of this woman, sex had been devalued by her involvement in prostitution. This was also the case for another woman:

See when I'm having sex with Marty he says, 'Lindy you jus' lie there.' I says I cannae help it. It must jus' be something inside me. Ye know I try, I do try ye know. I say, 'I'm tryin' as hard as you.' He says, 'You're no', Lindy, you're no'. . . .' So it's done something t'me inside as well.

It is of course difficult to disentangle the influence that personal biography and orientation towards sex might have on a prostitute woman's experience of sex in her private life. On the basis of these women's reports however it appears quite possible that selling sex could have a significant impact upon a woman's private relationships, whether narrowly considered in terms of the capacity to derive pleasure sexually, or more broadly, in terms of the influence this might have on the fabric of the relationship itself. Some women did report that sex with their private partners was negatively affected by having sold sex to others. This could be because of tiredness or feeling sore or just not being in the mood:

Actually see when you're workin' on the street and workin' the saunas it actually puts you off sex because sex jus' means money. Before I met Pat [her ex-boyfriend] I felt sex was cheap all the time, just a dirty feeling all the time 'cos of what you're doin'. You've got all these fuckin' men an' most of them are perverts. That's jus' the way I look at them.

Sheena felt that her sex life had been affected by prostitution: 'Yeah, I mean, because a lot of the time Sam is always wanting sex permanently but I don't feel like it, you know it just feels like another punter half of the time because I'm tired, I'm not interested. It's jus' like "come on, get on with it" kind of stuff. But I mean, I still, I didn't start enjoying sex 'til I was about 15, for women I suppose it's harder for them to work out how to enjoy it, you know, but, em, I do enjoy sex yeah but I mean a lot of the time

I can't be bothered with it. But I mean I reckon I've got a pretty healthy sex drive. I mean I like sex but em. . . .'

Whereas sex could come to be seen as something of a chore, or was devalued through their contacts with clients, the women highly valued non-sexual expressions of affection from partners or, in one case, from a sister. Affection-ate cuddles and kisses were of a completely different order to anything that they might experience with clients, which perhaps accounted for the great value placed upon them. Take for example the way in which one woman describes the difference between her relations with clients and with boy-friends:

See when I'm wi' ma boyfriend we go to bed and we do just that, we're under the covers, kissing and cuddling, and it's totally different.

Consider also the way in which Sheena contrasted the difference between sex with partners and the ease and comfort of snuggling up with her sister once work has finished for the evening:

Once I'm in the house I'm happy, if we're going back out, I get changed, washed and that . . . but, em, most of the time I just want to come in and settle down and Jane will sit down on this bed, half the time she ends up in my bed an' I don't get any peace, apart from when there's boyfriends round. . . . Yeah it's really warm in here in the evening, we've both heaters on we just snuggle up, watch telly and smoke fags and drink juice and eat, and eat and eat! And then go to sleep, I don't normally go to sleep till late.

Whether out of deference to the sensibilities of their partners or out of self-preservation, or a mixture of the two, the women were engaged in the delicate business of managing the presentation of themselves and their lives as uninfluenced by prostitution. Mostly this meant that the women either did not talk about their work or avoided the details of their contacts with clients. For some it also meant that they had to make sure their partners did not feel as if they were just clients (one reason why condoms are often ruled out in private relationships). Some women also reported feeling obliged to have sex with partners even though they did not feel inclined to. Although this feeling of obligation to meet the sexual needs of a partner is not exclusive to prostitutes, the sense of obligation may be more keenly felt where the woman is trying to preserve the impression of the relationship as being wholly distinct from prostitution. As Goffman (1959/1971) points out, managing the presentation of self is about trying to ensure that the impression conveyed is one that is consistent and compatible with the overall definition of the situation being fostered. However, he also goes on to note that the 'impression of reality fostered by a performance is a delicate fragile thing that can be shattered by very minor mishaps'. The women, in acting as if their involvement in prostitution did not have an impact on some of the most personal aspects of their lives and relationships, were placed in the position of having to be ever watchful of the possibility of contamination by prostitution. For at least some of the women, some of the time, keeping prostitution from adversely affecting their private lives could be like walking a knife edge.

The strategies that prostitutes use do not guarantee that they will be able to hold fast onto distinguishing commercial from private sexual encounters. In some senses it is worth considering the ability to make such a distinction as an ideal which was more or less achieved by prostitutes, more or less of the time. The factors influencing the achievement of this ideal related not only to the prostitute's personal state of mind but to her relationships with others. The stigma of being a prostitute did, to varying degrees, have an impact on private relationships with sexual partners as well as other family members. A particular area of latent and actual tension concerned the disjunction between selling sex to numerous men and normative conceptions of the sexually exclusive relationship.

Perhaps the most commonly experienced area of conflict lay in the management of relationships with private partners. Whereas the women themselves could, and with varying degrees of success did manage the distinction between clients and private partners, it often seemed that this was much more problematic for partners. There are two related issues here. The first concerns the social dichotomy of women into 'good' and 'bad' based on ideal notions of appropriate female behaviour. The second, not wholly unrelated, factor concerns the cultural expectation of sexual exclusivity in relationships, particularly as it relates to the behaviour of the female partner. The prostitute stands as the exemplar of the 'bad' woman, her evident unchastity marking her out for especial social derision (Pheterson 1988). As much as these social categories of acceptable and unacceptable mores of female behaviour are known by the women so too are they known by their partners. Some men clearly did find it very difficult to accept the fact of their partner prostituting:

> Leonie was usually to be found working with her friend Anna. We asked where she was and she explained that Anna's man had just come out of prison and objected to her working as a prostitute. 'He doesnae want her working down here, says he'll batter her if she does it again. He will too, he's already done it before when he found out she was down here. He keeps sayin' he's gonnae put it in the past but he keeps bringin' it back up again and punches her for it. Then he apologizes, and says he cannae sleep wi' her anymore. He says to me, I cannae understand how he feels cos she's his wife. It won't work out, it jus' won't because he cannae let go.'

The second related issue concerns societal notions of sexual exclusivity in relationships, particularly in so far as women are concerned. The value placed on monogamy is clearly at odds with women having many sex contacts, although it should be noted that many prostitutes would probably not see any contradiction here, since they generally perceive clients as irrelevant in so far as their personal lives are concerned. None the less for many of the women's partners the fact of prostitution had an undermining effect, causing resentment, jealousy, anger and sexual frustration. The following excerpts from interviews with two women serve to demonstrate the tensions that can surface:

> Melanie described the conflicts caused by her working. 'It causes a big problem aye, it causes a lot of arguments and then you're all frustrated,

you're shoutin' and bawlin' at one another and then it's like "oh you can spend time wi' your punters but you won't spend it wi' me" you know what I mean.'

Netta described her boyfriend's opposition to her working in the town. She has to hide all the evidence of it when she's at home (she has to hide all her condoms). He's always suspicious of her contact with men, wondering if they're clients; 'the taxi driver's only got to say t'me, "here you are hen" and me say "OK, thanks pal" and he'll be asking, "is he a punter, is he?" That's no' on, it's no' on at all, it's too much.'

Another woman described the general uncertainty her partner felt in so far as their sex life was concerned. It should be added however that this woman's partner was an injecting drug user while she herself was not. A substantial part of the daily cost of his drug habit was met through her prostitution. Meeting his financial needs (thereby obviating the necessity for him to earn money by means which could result in him having to serve a prison sentence if caught) had in fact been her initial motivation for starting to prostitute. Her partner's obvious financial dependence upon her may have been a factor influencing the guilt he professed to feel:

I mean there are times that I can feel the tension you know I can feel it and I'll say what's the matter and I know what's the matter . . . and we talk about it . . . we did have a lot of problems with our sexual relationship, because I was working and he felt guilty. Like, making a move to have sex with me he was, I don't know what came over him but it was as if when I'd been out there doin' it all night, 'you come home and that and I'd want you, to touch you'. He was scared I mean I couldn't understand why he could feel like that. . . . He doesn't do what I do, he can't understand what I'm actually doing whether I love somebody, you know, he doesn't know whether it's ooh, you know, and cuddles, but it's not.

Even the fact of prostituting to finance the drug habit of a partner was no guarantee of avoiding emotional conflict concerning sex contacts with clients. This woman commented apropos of her own life and experience of relationships with men:

She said she didn't think it necessary to tell any of her private partners that she worked as a prostitute. 'One guy I did tell, the guy who I'd moved to Fife with and he accepted it, but it was something that was always threw up in your face. . . . As I say, for most guys it is something that's very, very hard. I mean ye talk to any guy an' it's very hard for them to accept, even the junkies' boyfriends. You still see them ye know, the arguments between them, ye know what I mean. They still have them, even though ye know they [the women] are up there, they [their male partners] are getting their habit fed.'

One particularly sensitive area concerned pregnancy and issues of paternity. Most women used either oral or injectable contraceptives, to protect against pregnancy in their private relationships and as an additional precaution to the use of condoms with clients. None the less it is worth pointing out that the chaotic nature of many drug using women's lives has often meant that contraceptive use has been erratic and therefore potentially ineffective. Additionally there are women who are actively seeking to become pregnant by their private partners. Without the back-up of oral or injected contraceptives, a prostitute's main defence against becoming pregnant by a client has been the condom and perhaps also a spermicidal sponge. However, condoms do burst, and therefore it is at least possible that a woman might become pregnant through her sex contacts with clients. Most women would discount this possibility because of their use of condoms and other spermicidal agents but their partners may not share that same surety. This certainly appeared to be the case for the two women quoted below:

> Last night Leonie asked if we knew a certain woman. When we said we did she said she'd delivered a wee girl earlier that day. I then asked if she still had the same boyfriend. Leonie said that she did, she added that he didn't think the wean was his: 'He thinks it's a punter's.'

> Sal was describing how she'd been trying to fall pregnant for two years which meant not taking contraception beyond the condom. Her anxiety was that she might fall pregnant to a client. 'That would be hassle, I mean we even spoke about if I did fall pregnant, I was like, I can't blame him. I was angry and it did cause a lot of fights but he says, "I want blood testing to see if that baby is mine. . . ." I mean when he said that, I went crazy but then when I thought about it, I thought really I can't blame him I mean I can't. I mean what he flings at me, he doesn't understand what I do.'

Conclusion

This can be no more than a sketch of the various ways in which prostitutes appear to emotionally manage their contacts with clients and private partners. Common to the women was a desire to establish and retain a distinction between the provision of sexual services for a price and their consensual sexual relationships to which they attached meaning. The creation and maintenance of this distinction does however appear to be a much more complex, and dynamic, process than has sometimes been supposed. On reflection this is perhaps not surprising given the sophistication required to hive off areas of experience as discrete, particularly when one considers that it is the same body which is being used both as a saleable commodity and as a vehicle for sexual and emotional expression.

The energies which prostitutes put into retaining the distinction between commercial and private sex seem largely directed to the maintenance of meaning in their private relationships. The variety of these means of distinction is perhaps predictable given obvious differences in the temperaments and style of working of prostitutes. None the less whether a woman would refuse any kind of penetrative sex, or would not kiss, or would refuse oral sex, all seemed to be actively engaged in the same process of keeping clients at a distance. This was an understood and taken for granted objective among prostituting women. This distinction was however much harder for the women's private partners to make and sustain, even while they might be directly benefiting from her earning power as a prostitute. This could and did cause conflicts between men and women. Prostitution could be a powerful factor undermining the fabric of women's personal relationships.

The distinctions between private and commercial sex should perhaps not be seen as set in stone and absolute even though that may be what many prostitutes aspire to achieve. It seems as if prostitutes, and their partners, are engaged in a dynamic process of separating these domains of sexual and emotional experience, facilitated by the various mechanisms or rituals prostitutes use to distance clients from their emotional 'real' beings. Precisely because the boundaries between these domains have to be created and are not absolute, so they are more or less permeable at different times. Interpersonal relationships appeared to have most influence on efforts to retain commercial and private sex as discrete. Ironically while the fact of being emotionally and sexually involved with someone else further impressed the need to retain a clear distinction, it was apparently the case that private partners were most intent on undermining that distinction.

Part of the reason women hold themselves aloof from their commercial sex contacts concerns self-esteem. So also is it about the retention of meaning in their private lives. These are important reasons for wanting to assert the difference between being a prostitute and being a lover and help to explain the value they place on achieving that separation.

8

Conclusion

Introduction

Public anxieties and uncertainties over HIV infection were in large part the makings of this book. Were it not for public health concern over the potential role that prostitution might play in the spread of HIV, it is unlikely that our research would have attracted funding. This in itself is quite telling as it underlines the general perception that prostitutes are to be considered in terms of their impact on others. It is perhaps an irony of this study that by its end the focus on HIV infection was much less pronounced. Certainly the risks of HIV were no less serious a consideration, but then neither were the plethora of other risks that women had to face in the work they did. This shift in perception came as a result of spending time with the women in the red-light area. It was inevitable that we should reach a different appreciation of the experience of prostitution and accordingly come to consider the risks that prostitutes face in their work as well as the risks they are presumed to represent to others. It is this perspective which we hope has animated this book. As a conclusion to this book we want to consider the implications of this viewpoint in terms of service provision and afterwards consider the legal status of prostitution.

Service implications

Concern that female prostitutes may be spreading HIV has led to a massive expansion in services provided to prostitute women. In many cities within the UK, and elsewhere, night-time drop-in clinics and outreach services have been developed for prostitute women. The focus of the majority of these services has been on their sexual health. The reasons for this are as obvious as they are simplistic – prostitute women sell sex therefore they must be in need of sexual health services! In fact the needs of the women are likely to go way beyond HIV and sexual health. We saw in Chapter 6, for example, that violence to working women was a much greater risk to their health than HIV, since the likelihood of violent attack was much greater than was the likelihood of contracting HIV through sex work, particularly given the high levels of condom use. Yet how many of the services provided to women include provision for coping with the consequences of violent attacks by clients? Do they include the facility to offer the women legal advice or counselling in helping them to deal with the police in reporting such attacks? Also, given the proportions of street prostitutes using drugs, services should be able to respond to the multiple problems associated with drug abuse and drug injecting: overdoses, abscesses, hepatitis etc. Some of the services already provided to working women will already be doing this, while others will have a more narrow focus. Whatever the response, we have to avoid the easy assumption that prostitute women's needs have solely to do with sexual health matters.

HIV has been the moving force enabling the development of services to one of the most stigmatized groups in our society. However, the fact that HIV has not spread exponentially as was once feared, combined with increased pressures on public sector spending, may well translate into a reduced service for prostitutes. In such an event a valuable point of contact with a marginal sector of the population might be lost. Prostitutes are known not to make much use of conventional services; furthermore, such services are usually health-based and cannot cater for the plethora of prostitute concerns. The contact established between prostitute and service provider should be built upon in recognition of its value as a point of service delivery to an otherwise hard to reach population. The continued delivery of services to prostitutes should not be endangered on the basis of a reassessment of the extent of HIV among female prostitutes.

In our research we identified some women who were working as prostitutes and who were HIV positive. We need to consider what the response to such women ought to be. In some parts of the world, including parts of the US, there has been a resort to legal measures to stop HIV positive women from working (Woodhouse *et al.* 1993). Both from a practical and an ethical point of view such an approach seems neither feasible nor desirable. However there are also difficulties with the view that there is no problem where condoms are always used in sexual encounters. Such a response may have the advantage of being politically correct while not really grappling with the issue. From what we know about condom failure the recommendation to use a condom may be inadequate to protect the health of others. It may well be necessary to consider alternative ways whereby such women can support themselves, other than through resorting to prostitution. Such a suggestion may be anathema to some whose objection would be that one would then be rewarding people for becoming HIV positive. Aside from the fact that such a response fails to recognize the tragedy which HIV represents, it also fails to recognize that similar strategies are already employed in many countries. Health workers who are found to be HIV positive, for example, are found work in areas where the risks of HIV transmission are minimized. Do we support such a strategy for health workers but deny it for prostitutes because of our moral objection to the work that they do? Whatever one thinks of the suggestion of finding alternative sources of income or work for HIV positive women, it is important that the issues be confronted head on and furthermore that something is done about the situation, particularly in those countries where much higher levels of infection have been recorded. The option of imposing further legal control upon such women is likely only to force them into ever more covert styles of working.

Legalization, decriminalization or the status quo

In the remainder of this chapter we look at the various options in terms of the legal status of prostitution in the UK. Basically there are three options: legalization, the status quo, or decriminalization. Legalization would in effect mean that the job of prostitute became the same as any other job – teacher, doctor, plumber or solicitor. Prostitutes would be registered, they would probably work from certain locations (legalized brothels) and pay tax on the income they earned. Their health status would be periodically checked, and women could form a professional organization representing their interests and rights. Prostitutes, like any other group, could go on strike to improve their working conditions, fees etc. The strongest argument in favour of legalization is in essence that prostitution is no different from any other occupation and that to treat it as different is little more than a case of moral objection to the fact of women working. But this begs the question, is prostitution just like any other profession?

Nearly all of the women we interviewed began working as a prostitute because they felt they had to. This might be different for women working in brothels or in saunas or working as call girls. Some of the women were forced or inveigled into prostitution at a young age by men who knew the potential income they could earn. Others were forced by the desperation of their circumstances, whether through feeding a drug habit or feeding a family. On the streets the overwhelming majority of women we contacted had little education or trained job skills. Their opportunities for earning money legitimately were mostly limited to the long hours and low pay earned in most unskilled occupations. In these circumstances many women felt that they had no real choice but to prostitute. The lack of choice which many of these women felt has to be entered into the equation when one is considering the arguments for and against legalization. It is easy to argue that any woman should be allowed to do whatever she chooses with her body. The force of that argument is not in doubt; however, one cannot ignore the fact that very many women were working as prostitutes not because they chose to, but because they could see no alternative. We asked the women what they thought their reaction would be if their own child were considering working as a prostitute. The response from the women was always the same – they might not be able to stop their child but they would do all within their power, and then some, to try and prevent such an outcome. The unanimity of the women's reaction to that question tells us that they, more than anyone else, know that prostitution is not the same as any other job. They know the risks, the cost, and the reality of what the job entails and they did not want their loved ones to face what they had faced or to have to make the same choice that they had made.

The issue of exploitation can never be very far from any discussion of the legalization of prostitution (Hepburn 1993). There are those who say that it is the client not the prostitute who is exploited – she after all is well paid for her labours. Aside from the fact that many women are not well paid, it is not the client who is insulted, beaten, raped and murdered, arrested, fined or imprisoned. It is not the client who risks eviction if he takes a prostitute home with him, or who is seen as the pariah, spreading HIV and other sexually transmitted diseases among society's innocents. It is the prostitute who faces every one of these things every working day of her life and probably long after she has stopped working if the fact of her having worked becomes known about. Legalization would change some of these things but it would not change others. It would hold out the prospect of street prostitutes moving to work in legalized brothels but would it mean that the women would earn more money or would it mean that others would find it easier to earn money from the prostitute? The English Collective of Prostitutes have rejected calls for the creation of legalized brothels, believing that this would increase rather than decrease the exploitation of prostitute women (Lopez-Jones 1992).

But what of the women themselves? Some of the women we interviewed said that they would welcome such a change believing that it would allow them to work in the open with greater safety. There were others who said that such a move would increase the numbers of women working and would therefore increase competition in their work. There were some women who said that the payment of taxes would be no different to the fines they had to pay under their present circumstances, others who said that they would refuse to pay the tax man for the money they earn with their bodies. The clients expressed a similar range of views. Most of the clients said that they would welcome legalization; however, there was a significant minority of men who said that they did not feel prostitution should be legalized since this might increase the number of young girls on the streets earning money. Some of the clients said that they would be quite happy to visit state run and registered brothels, while others said they would continue to buy sex on the streets even if such brothels were available.

In terms of the status quo, although technically speaking prostitution itself is not illegal in the UK, it is so surrounded by legal restrictions covering such things as soliciting, the running of a brothel etc. as to be illegal in all but name. It is generally accepted that vigorous policing will never remove prostitution; it may make it less visible but it will not make it disappear. The status quo also places women in the position where they may be arrested at any time, fined, and forced to go back out on to the streets to pay those fines. It also makes them marginal members of society plying their trade within the hidden areas of night-time city life. The status quo increases the risks of violence which such women face and makes it that much more difficult to deliver the appropriate health and other services which such women need. For these reasons the status quo is probably the worst of the three options.

Decriminalization is the halfway house between the two options. It would entail no official change in the legal status of prostitution but an acceptance on the part of the authorities, including the police, of the women's work. Such an acceptance would probably entail the designation of certain areas of the city, or certain houses within those areas, where the women could work. The police would continue to have responsibility for those areas though they might adopt a low-profile presence. Any clients attacking women would be arrested and prosecuted and various of the health and legal advisory services could easily be made available to the women working in those areas. Of the options we have discussed our own recommendation would be for the decriminalization of prostitution.

Legal changes if they are to come, and they may well not, are only part of the story. To change the legal status of prostitution in our society will entail a much larger change in our attitudes towards sex in general and prostitution in particular. That change in attitude will only come about once we see the individuals involved in the world of prostitution as people rather than as the subjects of tabloid headlines and armchair moralizing. We hope that our descriptions in this book will help the process of demythologizing prostitution and enable a more open discussion to take place of our attitudes towards those who sell and buy sex. We also hope to have countered the assumption that just because a woman sells sex she somehow gives up her right to be treated as a human being.

Bibliography

Alary, M. and Worm, A. (1993) Risk behaviours of female prostitutes from Copenhagen, *PO-D09–3647 International Conference on AIDS*, Berlin 1993.

Amaro, F., Dantas, A. and Teles, L. (1995) Sexual behaviour in the city of Lisbon, *International Journal of STD and AIDS*, 6: 35–41.

Aral, J. (1993) Heterosexual transmission of HIV: the role of other sexually transmitted infections and behaviour in its epidemiology prevention and control, *Annual Review of Public Health*, 14: 451–67.

Barnard, M. (1992) Working in the dark: researching female street prostitution, in H. Roberts (ed.) *Women's Health Matters*. Routledge: London.

Barnard, M. (1993) Violence and vulnerability: conditions of work for streetworking prostitutes, *Sociology of Health and Illness*, 15: 683–705.

Barnard, M., McKeganey, N. and Leyland, A. (1993) Risk behaviours among male clients of female prostitutes, *British Medical Journal*, 307: 361–2.

Berry, S., Kanouse, D., Duan, N. and Lillard, L. (1992) Risky and non-risky sexual transactions with clients in a Los Angeles probability sample of female street prostitutes, *POD 5604 VIII International Conference on AIDS/III STD World Congress*, Amsterdam 1992.

Bhave, G., Wagle, V., Dejai, S., Handel, J. and Hearst, N. (1992) HIV–2 prevalence in prostitutes in Bombay, *POC 4623 VIII International Conference on AIDS/III STD World Congress*, Amsterdam 1992.

Bloor, M. (1995) *The Sociology of HIV Transmission*, London: Sage Publications.

Buma, A., Veltink, R., Vanameijden, E. *et al.* (1995) Sexual behaviour and sexually transmitted diseases in Dutch marines and naval personnel on a United Nations mission in Cambodia, *Genitourinary Medicine*, 71: 172–5.

Carr, S., Green, J., Goldberg, D., Cameron, S. *et al.* (1992) HIV prevalence among female street prostitutes attending a health-care drop-in centre in Glasgow, *AIDS*, 6(12): 1553–4.

Celentano, D., Nelson, K., Suprasert, S., Wright, N. *et al.* (1993) Behavioral and sociodemographic risks for frequent visits to commercial sex workers among Northern Thai Men, *AIDS*, 7(12): 1647–52.

Chaisiri, N., Danutra, V. and Limanonda, B. (1993) Prevalence of syphilis and anti-HIV–1 seropositive among prostitutes in two urban areas of Thailand, *PO-C14–2896 International Conference on AIDS*, Berlin 1993.

Chesler, P. (1978) *About Men*, New York: Simon and Schuster.

Corwin, A., Olson, J., Omar, M., Razaki, A. *et al.* (1991) HIV–1 in Somalia: prevalence and knowledge among prostitutes, *AIDS*, 5(7): 902–4.

Dada, A., Oyewole, F., Onofowokan, R. *et al.* (1993) Lagos, Nigeria, New Delhi HIV connection among high class prostitutes, *PO-C07–2744 International Conference on AIDS*, Berlin 1993.

Day, S. (1988) Prostitute women and AIDS: anthropology, *AIDS*, 2: 421–8.

Day, S., Ward, H. and Harris, J. (1988) Prostitute women and public health, *British Medical Journal*, 297: 1585.

Day, S. (1990) Prostitute women and the ideology of work in London, in D.A. Feldman (ed.) *Culture and AIDS*, New York: Praeger Publishers.

Day, S., Ward, H. and Perrotta, L. (1993) Prostitution and risk of HIV: male partners of female prostitutes, *British Medical Journal*, 307: 359–61.

de Graaf, R. (1995) *Prostitutes and their clients. Sexual Networks and Determinants of Condom Use*. Amsterdam: Ponsen and Looijen BV Wageningen.

de Graaf, R., Vanwesenbeeck, I., van Zessen, G. *et al.* (1993) The effectiveness of condom use in heterosexual prostitution in the Netherlands, *AIDS*, 7: 265–9.

de Meis, C., de Vasconnellos, A., Linhares, D. and Andradaserpa, M. (1991) HIV–1 infection among prostitutes in Rio de Janeiro, *AIDS*, 5(2): 236–7.

De Vincenzi, I., Braggiolli, L., El-Amri, M., Ancelle-Park, R. and Brunet, J. (1992) HIV infection in a population of prostitutes in Paris, *Bulletin-Epidemiologique-Medomadaine*, 47: 223–4.

Delacoste, F. and Alexander, P. (1988) *Sex Work: Writings by Women in the Sex Industry*. London: Virago Press.

Delaporte, F., Laga, M., Nzila, N., Goeman, T. *et al.* (1992) Risk factors for HTLV 1/11 infection in prostitutes and pregnant women in Zaire, *POC 4389 VIII International Conference on AIDS/III STD World Congress*, Amsterdam 1992.

Dobash, R. and Dobash, E.R. (1979) *Violence Against Wives: A Case Against the Patriarchy*. London: Open Books.

Espinoza, P., Egger, M., Gorter, A., Herrmann, B. *et al.* (1993) Low incidence of AIDS in Nicaragua: why and for how much longer, *PO-C06–2703 International Conference on AIDS*, Berlin 1993.

Estébanez, P., Rua Figueroa, M., Aquilar, M., Fitch, K. *et al.* (1992) HIV prevalence and risk factors in Spanish prostitutes, *POC 4189 VIII International Conference on AIDS/III STD World Congress*, Amsterdam 1992.

European Working Group on HIV Infection in Female Prostitutes (1993) HIV infection in European female sex workers: epidemiological link with use of petroleum based lubricants, *AIDS*, 7(3): 401–8.

Faugier, J., Hayes. C. and Butterworth, C. (1992) *Drug using Prostitutes, their Health Care Needs and their Clients*. Department of Nursing: University of Manchester, Manchester.

Fay, O., Viglianio, R., Taborda, M., Fernandez, E. *et al.* (1992) HIV surveillance among different communities in Argentina after 4 years surveillance, *POC 4064 VIII International Conference on AIDS/III STD World Congress*, Amsterdam 1992.

Fernandes, M., Reingold, A., Hearst, N., Inglesi, E. *et al.* (1992) HIV in commercial sex workers in Sao Paulo, *POC 4190 VIII International Conference on AIDS/III STD World Congress*, Amsterdam 1992.

Fields, A. and Walters, J. (1985) Hustling: supporting a heroin habit, in B. Hanson, G. Beschner, J.M. Walters and E. Bovelle (eds) *Life with Heroin, Voices from the Inner City*. Lexington, MA: Lexington Books.

Fitch, K., Rua Figueroa, M., Aquilar, M., Estébanez, P. *et al.* (1992) Sexual behaviour and condom use among Spanish prostitutes, *POD 5621 VIII International Conference on AIDS/III STD World Congress*, Amsterdam 1992.

Fowke, K., Anzala, O., Simonsen, J. *et al.* (1992) Heterogeneity in susceptibility to HIV–1 in continuously exposed prostitutes, *POC-4026 VIII International Conference on AIDS/III STD World Congress*, Amsterdam 1992.

Frischer, M.J. (1992) Estimated prevalence of injecting drug use in Glasgow, *British Journal of Addiction*, 87: 235–43.

Frohmann, L. (1991) Discrediting victim's allegations of sexual assault: prosecutorial accounts of case rejections, *Social Problems*, 38(2): 213–26.

Goffman, E. (1959/1971) *The Presentation of Self in Everyday Life*. London: Penguin Press.

Goffman, E. (1963/1970) *Stigma: Notes on the Management of Spoiled Identity*. London: Penguin Press.

Gorter, A., Esperanza, M., Davey-Smith, G., Octells, P. and Low, N. (1993) How many people actually use condoms? An investigation of motel clients in Managua, *Social Science and Medicine*, 36(12): 1645–47.

Gossop, M., Powis, B., Griffiths, P. and Strang, J. (1995) Female prostitutes in South London – use of heroin, cocaine and alcohol and their relationship to health risk behaviours, *AIDS Care*, 7: 253–60.

Green, S., Goldberg, D., Christie, P. *et al.* (1993) Female streetworker-prostitutes in Glasgow: a descriptive study of their lifestyle, *AIDS Care*, 5: 321–35.

Harcourt, C. and Philpot, R. (1990) Female prostitutes, AIDS, drugs and alcohol in New South Wales, in M. Plant (ed.) *AIDS, Drugs and Prostitution*. London: Routledge.

Harcourt, C. (1994) Prostitution and public health in the era of AIDS, in R. Perkins, R. Sharp, F. Lovejoy and G. Prestage (eds) *Sex Work and Sex Workers in Australia*. Sydney: University of New South Wales Press.

Hausser, D., Zimmerman, E., Dubois-Arber, F. and Paccaud, F. (1991) *Evaluation of the AIDS Prevention Strategy in Switzerland, Third Assessment Report, (1989–1990)*. Lausanne: Institut Universitaire de Médecine Sociale et Preventive.

Hepburn, M. (1993) Prostitution: Would legislation help?, *British Medical Journal*, 307: 1370–71.

Hochschild, A.R. (1983) *The Managed Heart: Commercialization of Human Feeling*. Berkeley: University of California.

Hoffman, B., Wallace, J., Steinberg, A., Weiner, A. *et al.* (1992) The high HIV incidence in New York City streetwalkers may have peaked in 1990, *POC 4660 VIII International Conference on AIDS/III STD World Congress*, Amsterdam 1992.

Holland, J., Ramazanoglu, C., Scott, C., Sharpe, S. and Thomson, R. (1992) Risk, power and the possibility of pleasure: young women and safer sex, *AIDS Care*, 4(3): 273–83.

Holzman, H. and Pines, S. (1982) Buying sex: the phenomenology of being a john, *Deviant Behaviour: An Interdisciplinary Journal*, 4: 89–116.

Horowitz, R. (1981) Passion, submission and motherhood: the negotiation of identity by unmarried inner city Chicanas, *The Sociological Quarterly*, 22: 241–52.

Hunt, D. (1990) Drugs and consensual crimes: drug dealing and prostitution, in M. Tonry and J. Wilson (eds) *Drugs and Crime*. Chicago: University of Chicago Press.

Inciardi, J., Lockwood, D. and Pottieger, A. (1993) *Women and Crack – Cocaine*. New York: MacMillan Publishing.

James, A. (1986) Learning to belong: the boundaries of adolescence, in A. Cohen (ed.) *Symbolising Boundaries: Identity and Diversity in British Cultures*. Manchester: Manchester University Press.

Jana, S., Chakraborty, A., Chatterjee, B., van Dam, C. *et al.* (1993) Knowledge, attitudes of CSW's towards STD/HIV and prevalence of STD/HIV among CSWs, *WS-C08–4 International Conference on AIDS*, Berlin 1993.

Johnson, A., Wadsworth, J., Wellings, K. and Field, J. (1994) *Sexual Attitudes and Lifestyles*. Oxford: Blackwell.

Kanouse, D., Berry, S., Duan, N., Richwald, G. *et al.* (1992) Markers for HIV–1, hepatitis B and syphilis in a probability sample of street prostitutes in Los Angeles County, California, *POC 4192 VIII International Conference on AIDS/III STD World Congress,* Amsterdam 1992.

Khabbaz, R., Darrow, W., Hartley, J. *et al.* (1990) Seroprevalence and risk factors for HTLV I/II infection among female prostitutes in the United States, *Journal of American Medical Association,* 263: 60–4.

Kihara, M., Imai, M., Kondoh, M., Watanabe, S. *et al.* (1993) HIV and hepatitis C virus infections among Japanese female prostitutes, *PO-C08–2772 International Conference on AIDS,* Berlin 1993.

Kitabu, M., Maitha, G., Mungai, J., Plummer, F. *et al.* (1992) Trends and seroprevalence of HIV amongst four population groups in Nairobi in the period 1989–1991, *POC 4018 VIII International Conference on AIDS/III STD World Congress,* Amsterdam 1992.

Kosia, A., Stevens, T. and Karbo, A. (1993) Epidemiology of HIV–2 in Sierra Leone, *PO-C07–2752 International Conference on AIDS,* Berlin 1993.

Lamothe, F., Bruneau, J., Soto, J., Lachance, N. *et al.* (1993) Behaviour of male and female intravenous drug users involved in prostitution in Montreal Quebec, Canada, *PO-D09–3648 International Conference on AIDS,* Berlin 1993.

Lewis, D. (1985) *The Prostitute and Her Clients: Your Pleasure is Her Business.* Illinois: Charles C. Thomas Publishers.

Leyland, A., Barnard, M. and McKeganey, N. (1993) The use of capture-recapture methodology to estimate and describe covert populations: an application to female streetworking prostitutes in Glasgow, *Bulletin de Méthodologie Sociologique,* 38: 52–73.

Lopez-Jones, N. (1992) Legalising brothels, *New Law Journal,* 1: 594–5.

Mastro, T., Limpakarnjanarat, K., Utaivorawit, V. *et al.* (1993) Decrease in chlamydia and gonorrhea in a cohort of female prostitutes in Northern Thailand, *PO-C03–2607 International Conference on AIDS,* Berlin 1993.

McKeganey, N. (1994) Why do men buy sex and what are their assessments of the HIV related risks when they do? *AIDS Care,* 6: 289–301.

McKeganey, N. and Barnard, M. (1992) Selling sex: female street prostitution and HIV risk behaviour in Glasgow, *AIDS Care,* 4(4): 395–407.

McKeganey, N., Barnard, M. and Bloor, M. (1990) A comparison of HIV-related risk behaviour and risk reduction between female street working prostitutes and male rent boys in Glasgow, *Sociology of Health and Illness,* 12: 247–92.

McKeganey, N., Barnard, M., Leyland, A., Coote, I. and Follet, E. (1992) Female street-working prostitution and HIV infection in Glasgow, *British Medical Journal,* 305: 801–4.

McKeganey, N., Barnard, M. and Bloor, M. (1994) How many prostitutes? Epidemiology out of ethnography in M. Boulton (ed.) *Challenge and Innovation: Methodological Advances in Social Research on HIV/AIDS.* London: Taylor and Francis.

McLeod, E. (1982) *Women Working: Prostitutes Now.* London: Croom Helm.

Miller, J. and Schwartz, M. (1995) Rape myths and violence against street prostitutes, *Deviant Behavior,* 16: 1–23.

Monny-Lube, P., O'Dell, E., Ngoumou, P. *et al.* (1993) Comparative HIV seroprevalence study among CSW's in Yacounde and Douala Cameroon, *PO-C31–3300 International Conference on AIDS,* Berlin 1993.

Morgan-Thomas, R., Plant, M.A., Plant, M.L. and Sales, D. (1989) Risks of AIDS among workers in the sex industry: some initial results from a Scottish study, *British Medical Journal,* 299: 148–9.

Morgan-Thomas, R. (1990) AIDS risks, alcohol, drugs and the sex industry: a Scottish study, in M. Plant (ed.) *AIDS, Drugs and Prostitution.* London: Tavistock/Routledge.

Mulhall, B., Hart, G. and Harcourt, C. (1995) Sexually transmitted diseases in Australia:

a decade of change, epidemiology and surveillance, *Annals Academy of Medicine Singapore*, 24: 569–8.

Multare, S., Mazzetti, M., Shinzato, R., Macias, J. *et al.* (1992) HIV prevalence among female prostitutes in Buenos Aires, *POC 4194 VIII International Conference on AIDS/III STD World Congress*, Amsterdam 1992.

Nzila, N., Laga, M., Thiam, M., Mayimona, K. *et al.* (1991) HIV and other sexually transmitted diseases among female prostitutes in Kinshasa, *AIDS*, 5(6): 715–21.

Onorato, M., Klaskala, W., Morgan, W. and Withum, D. (1992) High and rising HIV incidence in female sex workers in Miami, Florida despite stable HIV prevalence over time, *POC 4195 VIII International Conference on AIDS/III STD World Congress*, Amsterdam 1992.

Otido, J., Bwayo, J., Ndyinya-Achola and Plummer, F. (1993) Male regular clients of commercial sex workers, *PO-C14–2910 International Conference on AIDS*, Berlin 1993.

Pepin, J., Dunn, D., Gaye, I., Alonso, P. *et al.* (1991) HIV–2 infection among prostitutes working in the Gambia: association with serological evidence of genital ulcer diseases and with generalised lymphadenopathy, *AIDS*, 5(1): 69–76.

Perkins, R. and Bennett, G. (1985) *Being a Prostitute: Prostitute Women and Prostitute Men.* Sydney: George Allen and Unwin.

Pheterson, G. (1988) The social consequences of unchastity, in F. Delacoste and P. Alexander (eds) *Sex Work: Writings by Women in the Sex Industry.* London: Virago Press.

Pheterson, G. (1990) The category 'prostitute' in scientific enquiry, *The Journal of Sex Research*, 27: 397–407.

Philpot, C., Harcourt, C. and Edwards, J. (1991) A survey of female prostitutes at risk of HIV infection and other sexually transmissible diseases, *Genitourinary Medicine*, 67: 384–8.

Pickering, H., Todd, J., Dunn, D., Pepin, J. and Wilkins, D. (1992) Prostitutes and their clients: a Gambian survey, *Social Science and Medicine*, 34(1): 75–88.

Pickering, H., Quigley, M., Hayes, R. *et al.* (1993) Determinants of condom use in 24000 prostitute/client contacts in the Gambia, *AIDS*, 7: 1093–1098.

Pineda, J., Aguado, I., Rivero, A., Vergara, A. *et al.* (1992) HIV–1 infection among non-intravenous drug user female prostitutes in Spain: no evidence of evolution to pattern-II, *AIDS*, 6(11): 1365–9.

Potterat, J., Woodhouse, D., Muth, J. and Muth, S. (1990) Estimating the prevalence and career longevity of prostitute women, *The Journal of Sex Research*, 27: 233–43.

Rekart, M.L. (1993) Transsexuals and AIDS, *PO-C21–3101 International Conference on AIDS*, Berlin 1993.

Roberts, N. (1992) *Whores in History: Prostitution in Western Society.* London: Harper-Collins.

Rosenbaum, M. (1982) *Women On Heroin.* California: Rutgers University Press.

Rosenblum, L., Darrow, W., Witte, J., Cohen, J. *et al.* (1992) Sexual practices in the transmission of hepatitis B virus and prevalence of hepatitis delta virus infection in female prostitutes in the US, *Journal of American Medical Association*, 267: 2477–81.

Samarakoon, S. (1993) STD among female prostitutes attending the venereal diseases clinic in Colombo, Sri Lanka, *PO-C14–2891 International Conference on AIDS*, Berlin 1993.

Sanday, P. (1986) Rape and the silencing of the feminine, in S. Tomaselli, and R. Porter, (eds) *Rape.* Oxford: Basil Blackwell.

Savitz, L. and Rosen, L. (1988) The sexuality of prostitutes: sexual enjoyment reported by 'streetwalkers', *The Journal of Sex Research*, 24: 200–8.

Schoenfisch, S., Ellenbrock, T., Harrington, P., Bush, T. *et al.* (1993) Risks of HIV infection and behavioural changes associated with crack cocaine in pre-natal patients, *PO-C15–2920 International Conference on AIDS*, Berlin 1993.

Scully, D. (1990) *Understanding Sexual Violence: A Study of Convicted Rapists*. London: HarperCollins.

Scutt, J. (1992) The incredible woman – a recurring character in criminal law, *Women's Studies International Forum*, 15: 441–60.

Scutt, J. (1994) Judicial vision – rape, prostitution and the chaste woman, *Women's Studies International Forum*, 17: 345–56.

Shedlin, M. (1990) An ethnographic approach to understanding HIV high risk behaviour: prostitution and drug abuse, in C.J. Leukefeld, R.J. Battjes and Z. Amsel (eds) *AIDS and Intravenous Drug Use: Community Interventions and Prevention*. New York: Hemisphere Publishing Corporation.

Silbert, M. (1981) *Sexual Assault of Prostitutes*. San Francisco: Delancey Street Foundation.

Simonsen, J., Plummer, F., Ngugi, E., Black, C., Kreiss, J. *et al.* (1990) HIV infection among lower socio-economic strata prostitutes in Nairobi, *AIDS*, 4(2): 139–44.

Siraprapasiri, T., Thanprasertsuk, S., Rodklay, D., Srivanichakoun, S. *et al.* (1991) Risk factors for HIV among prostitutes in Chiang Mai, Thailand, *AIDS*, 5(5): 579–82.

Smith, J. (1993) *Misogynies*. London: Faber and Faber.

Smith, E. and Worm, A. (1993) HIV testing at the Danish STD clinics 1990–92, WS-C14–4 *International Conference on AIDS*, Berlin 1993.

Somma, V., Rivas, B. and Correa, M. (1993) Prostitution and AIDS in Uruguay, PO-D09–3669 *International Conference on AIDS*, Berlin 1993.

Stanko, E. (1985) *Intimate Intrusions: Women's Experiences of Male Violence, Rape, Child Sexual Abuse and Sexual Harassment*. London: Routledge.

Stimson, G. and Oppenheimer, E. (1982) *Heroin Addiction, Treatment and Control in Britain*. London: Tavistock.

Tabet, S., Darwin, L., Palmer, M., Williams, H. *et al.* (1992) Seroprevalence of HIV–1 and hepatitis B and C in prostitutes in Albuquerque, New Mexico, *American Journal of Public Health*, 82(8): 1151–4.

Taylor, A., Frischer, M., McKeganey, N. *et al.* (1993) HIV risk behaviours among female prostitute drug injectors in Glasgow, *Addiction*, 88: 1561–4.

Tirasawat, P., Ngaokaew, S., Absornthanasombat, T. *et al.* (1993) Spatial mobility of female commercial sex workers in Thailand, PO-D09–3652 *International Conference on AIDS*, Berlin 1993.

Traore-Ettiegne, V., Ghys, P., Diallo, M., Van-Dyck, E. *et al.* (1993) High prevalences of HIV infections and other STD in female prostitutes in Abidjan, WS-C08–3 *International Conference on AIDS*, Berlin 1993.

Valdespino, J., Garcia, M., Loo, E., Salcedo, R. *et al.* (1992) HIV–1 and STD sentinel surveillance among homosexual men and female prostitutes in Mexico, POC 4052 *VIII International Conference on AIDS/III STD World Congress*, Amsterdam 1992.

Vangelder, P. and Kaplan, C. (1992) The finishing moment – temporal and spatial features of sexual interactions between streetwalkers and car clients, *Human Organisation*, 51: 253–63.

Vanwesenbeek, I., de Graaf, R. and Visser, J. (1993) Protection styles of prostitutes' clients: intentions, behaviours and considerations in relation to AIDS, *Journal of Sex Education and Therapy*, 19: 79–92.

Vanwesenbeek, I., Van Zessen, G., de Graaf, R. and Straver, C. (1994) Contextual and interactional factors influencing condom use in heterosexual prostitution contacts, *Patient Education and Counselling*, 24: 307–22.

Vera, M., Alegria, M., Rivera, C., Robles, R. *et al.* (1992) STDs, HIV status and risk taking behaviour in female Hispanic sex workers, POC 4614 *VIII International Conference on AIDS/III STD World Congress*, Amsterdam 1992.

Wade, A., Dieng-Sarr, A., Diallo, A., Thiam, A. *et al.* (1993) HIV–1 and HIV–2 in Senegal, PO-C29–3264 *International Conference on AIDS*, Berlin 1993.

Ward, H., Day, S., Mezzone, J., Dunlop, L. *et al.* (1993) Prostitution and risks of HIV: female prostitutes in London, *British Medical Journal*, 307: 356–8.

Weller, S. (1993) A meta analysis of condom effectiveness in reducing sexually transmitted HIV, *Social Science and Medicine*, 36(12): 1635–44.

Woodhouse, D., Muth, J., Potterat, J. and Riffe, L. (1993) Restricting personal behaviour: case studies on legal measures to prevent the spread of HIV, *International Journal of STD and AIDS*, 4: 114–17.

Wong, M., Tan, T., Ho, M. *et al.* (1992) Factors associated with sexually transmitted diseases among prostitutes in Singapore, *International Journal of STD and AIDS*, 3: 332–7.

Wong, M., Archibald, C., Chan, R. *et al.* (1994) Condom use negotiations among sex workers in Singapore: findings from qualitative research, *Health Educational Research*, 9: 57–67.

Zapiola, I., Bouzas, M., Muchinik, G., Ladeda, V. *et al.* (1992) HIV–1 and HTLV 1/11 among prostitutes in Buenos Aires, Argentina, *POC 4661 VIII International Conference on AIDS/III STD World Congress*, Amsterdam 1992.

Index

Page numbers in italic indicate reference to a table or figure.